Praise for *Role Mate to Soul Mate*

"*Role Mate to Soul Mate* is the most practical love-enhancing book ever written. It will change your life."

> –Dr. John Gray, #1 *New York Times* bestselling author of
> *Men Are from Mars, Women Are from Venus*

"*Role Mate to Soul Mate* is a masterpiece. It incorporates powerful practices that will make you emotionally closer to your partner, children, family members, and colleagues."

> —Marci Shimoff, #1 *New York Times* bestselling author of
> *Happy for No Reason* and *Chicken Soup for the Woman's Soul*

"When the biological handcuffs leading to love slip away, Dr. Farrell helps couples transition from role mates to soul mates by reinventing our relationships and overcoming criticisms, complaints, and complacency."

> —Dr. Mehmet Oz, host of *The Dr. Oz Show*,
> and Lisa Oz, *New York Times* bestselling coauthors

"After savoring every word, I marveled, 'How can one book explode with so much wisdom, skills, and practical application?' If you are struggling to rediscover the chemistry, harmony, and love that once brought you together, *Role Mate to Soul Mate* is the essential read you will return to again and again. A *great* book."

> —Joneen Mackenzie, RN, BSN, president of the National Alliance
> for Relationship and Marriage Education (NARME)

"*Role Mate to Soul Mate* is much more than a book filled with wisdom; it is filled with more than twenty concrete practices that have proven the most effective for more than one thousand couples to translate that wisdom into a deeper, lifelong love. Read it. And experience it."

— John Mackey, cofounder of Whole Foods and author of *The Whole Story*

"When you read *Role Mate to Soul Mate*, you will experience why it is one of Esalen's most popular and transformative courses. For decades, Dr. Farrell invited all workshop participants to free follow-up group phone calls to report what worked and didn't work in real life. From this he developed more than twenty love enhancements and perhaps the most practical guide to love ever written."

— Michael Murphy, cofounder of The Esalen Institute
and coauthor of *The Life We Are Given*

"I have been a marriage and family therapist for more than fifty years and *Role Mate to Soul Mate* is the most important and helpful book I have ever read. It is the book I have wanted to give to my clients and the book I wish I had read when I was struggling in my own marriage. I know Warren practices what he preaches, and his own joyful family life is reflected in every page."

— Jed Diamond, PhD, LCSW, author of *The Enlightened Marriage*

"I doubt there's anybody on the planet who teaches couples communication better than Dr. Warren Farrell. Dr. Farrell is both an extraordinary original thinker plus among the most compassionate, kind, and wise human beings I've ever encountered. His *Role Mate to Soul Mate* book now allows every couple to benefit from these qualities to deepen their love."

— Kiril Sokoloff, chairman and founder of 13D Research
and author of *Personal Transformation*

"Each chapter is a treasure not only for its content, but also for the way it organizes intimacy into practical strategies with clarity and depth. Warren Farrell is a national treasure."

— Dr. Michael Gurian, *New York Times* bestselling author of
What Could He Be Thinking? and *Lessons of Lifelong Intimacy*

"We took Warren Farrell's relationship course, which became this magnificent book. We recommend both 100 percent if you want to transform the criticism and complaints in your relationship into opportunities to better love and be loved. *Role Mate to Soul Mate* is one of the most important books ever written about how to have a fulfilling romantic partnership."

—Annie Lalla, author of *Love Dojo*, and Eben Pagan,
relationship coaches, married partners, and parents

"Dr. Farrell guides us to take the practice, training, and conditioning we devote to our professional endeavors to the most important relationship in our lives. *Role Mate to Soul Mate* is invaluable."

—Clarence H. Carter, commissioner of
Tennessee Department of Human Services

"*Role Mate to Soul Mate* is packed with Dr. Farrell's seasoned wisdom and time-tested practical exercises that show us how to rekindle love by keeping criticism, complaints, control struggles, and complacency from eroding passionate connection. This book is a user's guide to feeling more appreciated, secure, and deeply loved."

—Dr. Richard A. Warshak, author of *Divorce Poison:
How To Protect Your Family from Bad-mouthing and Brainwashing*

"Among all the books and methodologies for resolving the blocks that kept us from fully loving each other, Warren's approach has created the most open and natural path for true intimacy between us. After 30 years together, his course and book have facilitated our falling in love with each other more deeply every day!"

—Peter Meyers, founder of Stand & Deliver and coauthor of *As We Speak*,
and Marcia Meyers, partner at Stand & Deliver

"This *Role Mate to Soul Mate* book and companion online course are the most important work being done in the world today to give couples the practical tools to become lifelong soul mates."

—Dr Marc Gafni, cofounder of the Center for World Philosophy and Religion
and author of *Your Unique Self*

"My soulmate of 55 years and I find the depth and thoroughness of Dr. Farrell's book and workshop to be the only lasting way to sustain or rekindle enduring love."

—Dr. Diane Sukiennik, author of *The Career Fitness Program*

"Warren's emotional expertise is a privilege to witness. To have a master like Warren walk you through the process of opening your own heart is a gift that will change your life forever."

—Annie Lalla, relationship coach and author of *Love Dojo*

"Role Mate to Soul Mate is the most powerful relationship 'software patch' ever created. It is like a combination of the *Tao Te Ching* and a repair manual. Warren Farrell must have sat under a tree and meditated on the nature of love for several lifetimes to achieve these insights—as much a revelation as a relationship book."

—Eben Pagan, relationship coach, husband, and father

"I highly recommend *Role Mate to Soul Mate* as a compelling guide to forge an authentic marriage or lifelong intimacy with incalculable rewards."

—Brad Wilcox, sociology professor and director of the
National Marriage Project at the University of Virginia

"Do you want to feel more deeply 'seen'—more lovingly held by your partner? Read this book! Use these innovative practices. Gift yourself with these incredibly effective and practical techniques.

We have. We know they work."

—Peter J Klaphaak, Jr., MD, and Jan Disanto, MFT

ROLE MATE to SOUL MATE

Also by Warren Farrell, PhD

The Boy Crisis: Why Our Boys Are Struggling and What We Can Do About It
(coauthored with John Gray)

The Myth of Male Power: Why Men Are the Disposable Sex

Why Men Are the Way They Are

Father and Child Reunion:
How to Bring the Dads We Need to the Children We Love

Women Can't Hear What Men Don't Say

Why Men Earn More: The Startling Truth Behind the Pay Gap–
and What Women Can Do About It

ROLE MATE to SOUL MATE

The Seven Secrets to Lifelong Love

Warren Farrell, PhD

BenBella Books, Inc.
Dallas, TX

BenBella Books, Inc.
10440 N. Central Expressway
Suite 800
Dallas, TX 75231
benbellabooks.com
Send feedback to feedback@benbellabooks.com

BenBella is a federally registered trademark.

Printed in the United States of America
10 9 8 7 6 5 4 3 2 1

Library of Congress Control Number: 2023054057
ISBN 9781637744567 (print)
ISBN 9781637744574 (ebook)

Editing by Claire Schulz
Copyediting by Ruth Strother
Proofreading by Denise Pangia and Cape Cod Compositors, Inc.
Indexing by WordCo Indexing Services
Text design and composition by Jordan Koluch
Cover design by Morgan Carr
Printed by Lake Book Manufacturing

To Liz for 30 years of ever-deepening love.
And to Gail, Erin, Alex, Hutch, and Finley

Author's Note

n this book, most individuals' names and identifying details have been changed, and stories are often integrations of multiple couples' experiences to protect privacy.

Since the Caring and Sharing Practice involves couples sharing privately with each other, many couples in my workshops do not share their experiences in the group. The examples in this book are drawn from couples who were so open as to share.

Contents

Acknowledgments

My first acknowledgment is to my wife, Liz. We met some 30 years ago and were in many ways in the "opposites attract" category. The "opposites" part contributed to our breaking up. But the "attract" part led us to using a rudimentary form of what would become the "Role Mate to Soul Mate" course and this book. I deeply acknowledge Liz for working with me toward hearing each other without being defensive and in the process discovering how we could combine our "opposites" to create a more empowered partnership and now a lifelong love. As a bonus, each step that deepened our love also deepened the course. Now I couldn't imagine my life—or this book—without either Liz or our continued use of this course.

Along with Liz's input, virtually every part of this book was enhanced by the couples who gave me feedback during the group phone calls one month and one year following each workshop.

It has always been my desire to make the "Role Mate to Soul Mate" course available to people who cannot afford to attend my workshops. This was made possible by creating an online video version of the workshop as a result of months of editing by Patrick Renfro. His editing allows each couple who watches to pause and do all the exercises while they also witness me guiding two couples through each step. I wish to acknowledge Annie Lalla, Eben Pagan, and Amy and Steve Carlson for making sure that everything I instructed worked for them in practice, and for their penetrating questions, which gave me an opportunity to make the video a powerful experience for any couple (see the Appendix for a QR Code to the course and warrenfarrell.com and click on the Couples' Communication tab for descriptions). I also acknowledge Jeff Page, a Christian minister, for using scripture to show how my online video version teaches couples to create in practice what scripture guides Christians to do.

I am continually appreciative of the dedicated team that Glenn Yeffeth, BenBella's founder and president, has both organized and inspired to give their best. I thank especially Claire Schulz, my editor, for her astute organizational skills to help me best translate the workshop, online video versions of *Role Mate to Soul Mate*, and early manuscript into a much clearer book.

Finally, I thank my assistant, Julia Roegiers, for her technical help and Gen Z perspective.

A Personal Introduction

Afte reading this personal introduction, you will be privy to the emotional and psychological building blocks from which *Role Mate to Soul Mate* evolved. These building blocks ultimately allowed me to help couples from being vulnerable to the Achilles' heel of humans: the inability to hear personal criticism from a loved one without becoming defensive.

On the surface, my passion for what evolved into *Role Mate to Soul Mate* would appear to have begun with my involvement with the issues of girls and women in the early 1970s, when I served on the board of directors of the National Organization for Women (NOW) in New York City. This was followed by my involvement with the issues of boys and men. I formed around 300 men's groups, and, more recently, wrote *The Boy Crisis*.

Initially it seemed obvious that, well, men are from Mars, and women are from Venus. However, same-sex partners in my workshops made it apparent that our inability to handle personal criticism from a loved one without becoming defensive is not specific to heterosexual couples. And the issue isn't just that couples are not feeling heard, but that they also feel they are walking on eggshells, fearing that if they bring up a concern, it would escalate into an argument and a counterattack. So what they would love to express becomes repressed.

And, of course, as our country and world became increasingly polarized, I saw that the only people who felt they were walking on eggshells were, well, women, men, children, parents, employers, employees, Republicans, Democrats, Russians, Ukrainians ... In brief, few people can handle personal criticism *or* even criticism of their ideas.

These more recent experiences, though, did not account for the derivation of my angst about these human tendencies. What would ultimately lead to *Role Mate to Soul Mate* probably gestated in my psyche in about ninth grade.

It was the McCarthy Era. I can recall asking in high school—apparently too frequently—why we weren't curious about the Soviet perspective on Communism and capitalism as well as our own. The reaction I received—even in the first year of high school—was McCarthy Era–type suspicion: was I one of them? At times this led me to doubt my thinking; at other times to repress it.

Later that year my dad was offered a position managing a company in the Netherlands, and our family moved from New Jersey to The Hague. My uncle managed some boats in Paris, across from les Bateaux Mouches on the Seine. When he invited me to be a cabin boy and assured my parents that both he and my slightly older cousin would watch out for me, they agreed to let me work on the boats during the summer.

As I came to trust my cousin, I cautiously mentioned to him my dislike of the McCarthy Era approach to Communism. He responded, "Oh yes, America and the Soviets are both bully nations. They both think they have all the answers, and they try to push their views on everyone else. They're not different; they're alike."

His perspective opened my mind in two ways: First, **just because my thinking is widely rejected doesn't mean it has no value.** Translation: *I* have value. I could feel an increase in my trust in myself.

Second, it planted the first seeds of what would become a growing disappointment in the human tendency to bond over a common enemy. I feared that bonding with someone over a common enemy means we have an incentive to *keep* the enemy an enemy. It was my first glimpse into what I now think of as our enemy dependency.

As I grew up, I saw the enemy dependency monster rearing its head all around me, especially with gossip: the more salacious the dirt about the outsider, the more everyone listening feels like an *insider*. I also began to experience how the people who attempted to bond with me by speaking negatively about others would soon say negative things about me to deepen their bond with someone else.

The good news? I avoided being seduced into bonding with a gossiper and therefore avoided being the next target of that gossiper. The downside? I began to feel a bit like a lone ranger.

In the late 1960s, as the women's movement surfaced, the male-female version of bonding based on the common enemy intensified. Some of my students at Rutgers University saw the early feminists as pioneers; others saw them as man-hating bra burners. I would facilitate my classes to first debate those with whom they disagreed. And then I required them to reverse roles. The "winners" were the ones best able to articulate the others' points of view.

While I was wary of the most active feminists' tendency to cast men and the patriarchy as the oppressors and be blind to the sacrifices many dads made to support their families doing jobs they didn't like, most of my personal sympathies were with the women's movement's goals to increase the flexibility of women's roles. I recalled that brilliant women in my high school were almost never encouraged to be scientists, CEOs, or future senators. And this also played out at home, where I saw how my sister, Gail, had an interest in boys whom she was not encouraged to ask out but to wait and hope. Both saddened me for the opportunities lost—for the women, the country, and the world. Oh yes, and to the boys who might have been afraid to ask out my sister for fear of rejection.

My students, seeing what one called "the fire in your belly when you talk about women's issues," inspired me to petition for a change in my doctoral dissertation to the psychology and politics of the women's movement. A caring professor on my dissertation committee at NYU warned, "Warren, the women's movement is just a fad. It's not worthy of a dissertation."

Fortunately, as this assessment was in process, I became an assistant to the president of NYU. Whether it was because of my passion, my persistence, or my new position, the professors who objected eventually gave me the green light.

The combination of my research and passion is what led to my serving on the board of directors of NOW in New York City. That experience led to my first book, *The Liberated Man*, which focused on introducing men to the value of liberated women. Even in that book, where 80 percent of the content focused on getting men to understand women's issues, I couldn't resist adding some of men's parallel perspectives. For example, that the male equivalent of being treated as a sex object was being treated as a success object.

Ironically, a conflict within NOW opened my mind to boys' and men's issues on a much more visceral level. NOW was conflicted as to whether it should continue allowing male membership, feeling that particularly during their once-per-month meetings of consciousness-raising groups, the presence of men often inhibited women from sharing their full range of feelings. Ultimately, NOW struck a deal: if I would form separate men's groups while the women were meeting, and if the women felt safer as a result, it would agree to continue letting men be members.

During the initial meetings of the men's groups, inspired by the fact that we had all self-selected to be at a meeting of NOW members, we mostly shared how we could be better male feminists. Since I was doing my dissertation on the topic, I felt I could justify adding some tidbit of my findings (a.k.a. give a minilecture). While I convinced myself that my intent was to inspire us to be better male feminists, it probably did more to inspire guilt as to why we weren't. Perhaps we were all just competing to be the biggest jock in the sensitivity group.

Around our fourth meeting, I experimented with a different approach. I asked the men, "As a boy or young man, what created the glint in your eye—maybe a sport; being a writer, musician, artist, or actor? Now compare that with what you are doing on an everyday level now."

Slowly the men opened up with stories of their aspirations as teenagers or in their early twenties versus the reality of disappointments they had never discussed with anyone. Many of them had never allowed themselves to even think about these disappointments until they heard the other men share their stories.

While this was true for all but the youngest of us, it was more markedly true for the dads who wanted their children to have opportunities they hadn't had, and to be able to afford homes in neighborhoods with good schools. They knew being a starving artist just wasn't going to accomplish that. One of the men, an elementary school teacher who loved kids but hated administration, had nevertheless agreed to become a principal so he could earn more.

Soon the men's groups were doing for me what the women's groups did for the women—they opened my mind and heart to the ways in which my socialization to be a man was limiting me. I realized I was less interested in becoming the president of NYU or another university than I was in being an author. Forming the men's groups and being on the board of NOW gave me something unique to write about for publications such as the *New York Times* and in my first book. That in turn led to speaking engagements that protected me from being a starving artist.

When I decided to form both men's and women's groups after each speaking engagement—ultimately some 300 men's and 250 women's groups—misunderstandings between the sexes became palpable. This led to my introducing communication skills into my workshops. Thirty years of feedback from these workshops gradually allowed me to create a practice for couples that deepened and sustained their love. But the process wasn't easy, as the Introduction will make apparent.

Introduction

M ost couples in my workshops have described their early relationship passion was too often followed by four depleters of
love: criticisms, complaints, feeling controlled, and experiencing complacency. This makes sense since falling in love is biologically
natural. However, sustaining love appears to be biologically unnatural.

Among the four depleters of love, the toughest to deal with, as I noted
in the personal introduction, is the ability to handle personal criticism
from our loved one without becoming defensive. Historically, criticism often signaled an enemy, and building defenses was functional for survival;
it is just dysfunctional for love.

When the men's and women's groups I formed met separately, they
felt heard and seen by those of their own sex. After a while, though, they
began to develop a bit of an attitude toward the other sex. So I began having the groups meet separately for only three months and then alternate
meeting together and separately after that. The three months of separate
meetings allowed each sex to feel safely heard, after which each sex was
more open to the other sex's feelings.

That need to feel heard *first* would become a seminal insight to a prerequisite to being able to hear criticism without becoming defensive. However, it was just the beginning of what it would take to both deepen love and sustain that depth for a lifetime. When I returned to campus a year or two after I had initially spoken, I experienced a second insight that would ultimately help me build the road from role mate to soul mate.

The Road from Role Mate to Soul Mate

I had taken pride in the standing ovations following my appearances. However, when I returned a year or two later, I experienced what comedians often experience—an immediately positive response and standing ovation, but few people remembering even one joke a day later. In contrast, I heard that the men's and women's groups were having more of an enduring palliative effect.

I sensed that my presentations might have a more enduring impact if I substituted talking to the audience with involving them. I began challenging my audiences to walk a mile in the other sex's shoes.

I first challenged the men: "Every woman is in a beauty contest every day of her life, so come on stage and be in a parallel men's beauty contest." Then I challenged the women to participate in a role reversal date: "Take just a few of the approximately 100 risks of sexual rejection that men often experience either in reality or in our mind."

The transitory impact of my lectures versus the often yearslong impact of my walk-a-mile-in-each-other's-shoes experiences informed the way I would eventually do my Couples' Communication workshops: less talking and insights, and more working with each couple to create a lifelong structure that would give them a way to walk a mile in each other's shoes every day of their lives.

By 1986, I began incorporating that into my workshops. I balanced my book *The Liberated Man*, which had a feminist perspective, with my next book, *Why Men Are the Way They Are,* which answered women's ques-tions about men. Rather than just explaining both sexes' divergent per-spectives, I focused one of five segments of my "Why Men Are the Way They Are" workshops on concrete methods of communicating that in-cluded methods of listening to each other.

I saw that the strategy of walking a mile in the other's shoes applied not only to male-female couples, but also to same-sex couples. As I de-fined a "couple" as any two people with a past who desire a future with better communication, I saw that a couple also included a parent and child, and an employer and employee. Oh yes, and even two family mem-bers passionate about their opposing political perspectives!

Then one day, still in the era of letters, if you will, I received a letter from a man who had been in a workshop I had conducted at Esalen, a re-treat center in Big Sur, California. He wrote that one of my five workshop segments—the one on couples' communication—had been so helpful to him that "I am now using it successfully in my family business." I imag-ined a family of four or five. And then I noticed the letter was signed by S. Robson Walton, son of Walmart's founder, Sam Walton. I knew enough to know that as the world's largest family business, Walmart could afford any of the myriad couples coaches in the world, so his letter felt affirming.

His letter came at a perfect moment. I had intuited that the workshop needed more than what the couples' communication segment was pro-viding. While couples had successfully practiced listening non-defensively during the workshop, too often I would hear weeks later that when one of them criticized their partner, their partner would nevertheless respond defensively. Soon what had started as a simple criticism escalated into a verbally abusive argument.

In brief, their practice of non-defensive listening in the workshop set-ting didn't come to the rescue when it was needed in real life. In real life, when criticisms appeared, the insights disappeared.

Since being defensive is biologically natural, and getting rid of our defenses is biologically unnatural, I envisioned that being truly receptive to our partner's criticisms would involve altering our biologically natural state. I doubted that could be done in any one lifetime, but I wondered if I could help couples create conditions where they could do it *temporarily.*

The next question was what those conditions might be. I experimented with having couples set aside just two hours each week during which each partner would psychologically prepare themselves for hearing just one of their partner's concerns. I came to call this set-aside time Caring and Sharing time.

This helped a lot. And I observed that it helped even more when the concern was preceded and followed by what each partner appreciated about the other. I came to call the whole process, with the appreciations at the beginning and end, a Caring and Sharing Sandwich. I found that two appreciations at the beginning combined with the anticipation of two at the end together created an emotional womb.

Until this point, the workshop was largely an adapted form of active listening with a good emotional womb. However, it still failed to *consistently* give couples the emotional security not to feel defensive while being criticized. I knew that unless a couple could consistently depend on their partner to feel secure—even more loved—while being criticized, they would still feel like they were walking on eggshells. I had to invent something that would ensure internal security even as the criticism was happening.

This was no easy task because in essence **I was asking the couples to create an evolutionary shift: to psychologically associate being criticized with an opportunity to be loved rather than attacked.**

I worked on creating meditations that I hoped when practiced together would substitute the biologically natural propensity for defensiveness with the anticipation of a deeper love. It took a quarter century to create six specific meditations that the highest percentage of couples found the most effective (see chapter 6, "Secret 2"), not just the meditations they found most effective during the workshop, but the ones they felt had proven most effective a month or two—and then a year or two—after the workshop. I discovered this by inviting every couple to a free group follow-up phone call a couple of months postworkshop, and then about a year after that.

These follow-up group calls gave me years of feedback as to what worked and what didn't. Since male-female issues are also central to my relationship with my wife, Liz Dowling (she let me keep my birth name!), she and I have been a testing ground since we first encountered our chemistry for each other more than 30 years ago.

From the follow-up calls (and my own personal experience), it soon became clear that any semblance of an evolutionary shift was temporary. For most people who are new to the practice, the altered mindset of associating being criticized with an opportunity to be more deeply loved lasts for only a half hour or so. Fortunately, with consistent practice and as new neurons begin firing in our brain, couples can extend the length of time they can associate being criticized with an opportunity to be more deeply loved. So this was clearly a discipline. The discipline of love.

I began to compare my weekend "Role Mate to Soul Mate" retreats to weekend exercise retreats: After the participants had practiced the exercises together, everyone felt rejuvenated and promised themselves they'd make this part of their everyday life. But only some did. Life got in the way. (I felt a bit sad about that until I looked within and noticed how I have to exert discipline every day to stop writing this book to take a hike or do yoga! Or even to practice Caring and Sharing.)

The underlying secret is that making the evolutionary shift from the biologically natural process of falling in love to the unnatural process of sustaining and deepening love requires both art and discipline. Discipline and love don't sound like they go together. In this book, it will be clear why they are inseparable for the journey from role mate to soul mate.

The Most Effective Use of This Book Is ...

Role Mate to Soul Mate is most effective in deepening love when used as a companion guide while viewing the online video version of my couples' communication course. I feel so strongly about this that I created an Appendix with a QR code that will allow you to have the course for more than 50 percent off ($97), so that the least expensive way to access the course is to have this book in your hand! The online course allows you and your partner to participate in the process as you observe me guiding two couples through the course. You can pause as the couples do the exercises so you can work through challenges similar to theirs. Watching me help them will also help you.

The book version of the "Role Mate to Soul Mate" course emerged because many couples had questions that required more in-depth answers than the time allotted in either the online video course or my live workshops. Chapter 1, for example, answers questions such as if our communication is better than our parents' and grandparents', why is our generation more likely to divorce? In the book, I explain why, as well as what you and your partner can do to both improve communication and reduce the likelihood of divorce. Similarly, in Part IV, "From Civil War to Civil Dialogue," I share how you can modify the book's relationship skill sets to apply them to friends, colleagues, other family members, political opponents—virtually everyone in your life who has not taken the course.

Acknowledging the Pioneers

Role Mate to Soul Mate does not replace a good therapist, who can help undo the dysfunctions emanating from family backgrounds or prior traumatic life experiences. Nor does it replace the excellent contributions made by devoted couples' therapists such as John and Julie Gottman, John Gray, Harville Hendrix and Helen LaKelly Hunt, Gay and Kathlyn Hendricks, and Esther Perel (whose ideas I reference in chapter 1).

My wife, Liz, and I, have benefitted from Gottman's *Seven Principles for Making Marriage Work* and enjoyed exercises such as his Love Maps. And as someone who has taken more than 600 walks and done multiple presentations with John Gray, I have witnessed how his ability to articulate that the way men and women think and behave can lead both sexes—especially once they have children—to feel less alone, more compassion for each other, and more likely to laugh at themselves.

Similarly, I have learned from Gay and Kathlyn Hendricks's *Conscious Loving*. And the contributions of Harville Hendrix and the late Helen LaKelly Hunt in their creation of Imago Relationship Therapy has made many couples aware of how their choice of partners was influenced by their family history, and has introduced them to active listening and empathy.

The purpose of *Role Mate to Soul Mate* is to add to the lifetime contributions of these couples' therapists.

The more the ideas in this book are new and creative for you, the faster you will forget them: memory benefits from context; creativity is creative in part because it has little context. Toward the end of the book, I'll have you do a ceremony with your partner that will be assisted by reviewing what you most wish to retain. So underline and keep a notebook.

Role Mate to Soul Mate is divided into four parts. In part I, "Foundational Wisdom," I outline the 15 differences between role mates and soul mates, and introduce the 23 Love Enhancements that facilitate becoming a soul mate. I introduce four common Depleters of Love, or the Four Cs: criticism, complaining, control, and complacency. We'll look at why we are often oblivious to our own participation in the Four Cs and how insidious they are in undermining a relationship. I'll share the top ten foundational wisdoms that I've found to be most helpful for almost all couples and explain how all ten of those foundational wisdoms temporarily disappear when criticism appears. Then I will discuss an eleventh foundational wisdom: the Power of Wisdom Paradox. Finally, you'll articulate to your partner the answer to key questions about the nature of your love, your key challenges with each other, and the different styles of each of your defenses.

In part II, "The Seven Secrets to a Deeper Love," I share seven of the core secrets to overcoming the barriers to deeper love. They are:

Secret 1—Appreciations and gratitude: panning for your partner's gold, and panning for the gold in life

Secret 2—The Caring and Sharing Practice: how to handle personal criticism without becoming defensive

Secret 3—Creating and sustaining a Conflict-Free Zone, including the Four-Part Apology

Secret 4—The magic of the Ask

Secret 5—Couples who play together stay together: bonding via play, whimsies, dancing, roughhousing, and teasing

Secret 6—Creating win-win solutions to your stickiest problems

Secret 7—Creating family dinner nights so they don't become family dinner nightmares

In part III, "Living in Love," I offer concrete ways of changing the energy in your home from complacency to memories of being appreciated no matter where in your home you wander. We'll explore how to avoid the Four Lazinesses that often set in after beginning to practice these teachings, and how to reverse the damage. You'll create a well-thought-out commitment to change and a renewal of vows in an artistic and memorable way that will also require the discipline of following through with the change to which you have committed.

In part IV, "From Civil War to Civil Dialogue," we'll look at how we can adapt the relationship skills that help us transition from role mate to soul mate to a skill set applicable to the rest of the world via making a transition from civil war to civil dialogue. You'll learn to apply this modified skill set to your parents and children, to colleagues and friends, and even to political adversaries!

While there are few things more rewarding than becoming soul mates and having a secure path to reversing any setback, there is something that can even undermine couples who have made significant progress. That's the "Higher Expectations Trap." So let's clear that up first.

Part I

FOUNDATIONAL WISDOM

Chapter 1

Averting the Higher Expectations Trap with an Evolutionary Shift

When I ask the couples in my "Role Mate to Soul Mate" workshops to raise their hands if they think they communicate better than their parents or grandparents, about 90 percent of the hands go up. (About 5 percent aren't paying attention!)

If better communication is more prevalent, why are divorces more prevalent? Why are couples in my workshops nevertheless more likely than their parents and grandparents to make the journey from courtship to a court of law?

Consider the Higher Expectations Trap. Historically, a primary goal of marriage was to ensure survival. To survive, a couple played roles: she raised children; he raised money. Couples today can pursue something their parents or grandparents didn't have the time or money—that is, the luxury—to pursue: the higher expectations of being *soul* mates.

These higher expectations have upsides and downsides. Many couples may communicate better than their parents do, but these couples are often critical of each other when the soul-mate goals described below are only partially met.

Psychological Divorce and the Minimum-Security-Prison Marriage

We say that love makes the world go round and our marriage vow is 'til death do us part, but even the 50 percent of couples who remain legally married often feel psychologically divorced. Their partner makes a suggestion, they experience it as criticism, and they respond defensively. Soon it's a full-blown argument and they're feeling more alienation than love.

Couples with children often feel so overwhelmed with responsibilities and fatigue they have neither the time nor the energy to process their resentments. At some point one or both partners' volcano erupts, or they emotionally withdraw and mechanically march through their daily obligations. Unless things are terrible, they feel that for the stability and security of the children, they should remain married. They often feel they are in what might be called a minimum-security-prison marriage.

If a psychological divorce describes your marriage—or your nonmarital relationship—know that although you can solve the problem, you are not the underlying cause. The underlying cause is what I call the love trap: falling in love is biologically *natural*; sustaining love is biologically *unnatural*. Who set this trap?

Throughout history, when another tribe, kinship network, or country criticized us, we feared it was a potential enemy. Building our defenses was functional for survival. (Or we killed the criticizer/potential enemy before they killed us.) Evolutionarily, the Achilles' heel of human beings is our inability to handle personal criticism without becoming defensive.

Role Mate to Soul Mate	
Role Mate Survival Roles	**Soul-Mate Fulfillment Goals***
Division of roles	Flexibility of roles
Women and men marry to create a whole	Whole persons partner to create synergy
Woman raises children; man raises money	Both sexes raise children; both sexes raise money
Children obligatory	Children a choice
Woman expected to risk life in childbirth; man expected to risk life in war or to protect family	Childbirth rarely life-threatening; war a choice; both sexes check out the burglar
Sex for procreation or to meet man's needs	Sex for mutual fulfillment
Neither party can end contract	Either party can end contract
Women as property; men expected to die before "property" was hurt	Sexes equally responsible for self and other
Both sexes subservient to needs of family	Both sexes balance needs of family with needs of self
Love emanates from mutual dependence	Love emanates from a compatibility of soul and values
Love *less* conditional (till death do us part)	Love *more* conditional (e.g., no abuse; expectations of happiness; mutual respect)
Choice of Partners	
Parental influence is primary	Parental influence is secondary
Women expected to marry their source of income (marry up)	Neither sex expected to provide more than half the income
Premarital Conditions	
Men addicted to female sex and beauty, then deprived of "fix" until they supply security	Neither sex more addicted or deprived than the other**

* Most of these goals are "in process."

** For most couples, this goal is far from being achieved.

Source: Updated from *The Myth of Male Power* by Warren Farrell, PhD.

The problem? **Building defenses was functional for survival; it is just dysfunctional for love.**

Soul-mate love, then, requires an evolutionary shift in the way we handle personal criticism. Why? Because the more we love someone, the more vulnerable we feel. The more vulnerable we feel, the more the criticism hurts. If the criticism is given badly, it hurts more. (And all criticism from a loved one is perceived as given badly!)

The secret to feeling soul-mate love is feeling understood. **No one says, "I want a divorce, my partner understands me."** Our natural propensity to become defensive cuts our partner off from feeling understood. When we criticize our dog, our dog doesn't get defensive. We rarely hear, "I want a divorce from my dog."

When our partner anticipates defensiveness, they fear bringing up their concerns. Soon they are walking on eggshells. The love fades.

Since *Role Mate to Soul Mate* is about the unnatural process of sustaining love, most everything you will learn will feel unnatural. Sustaining love requires the discipline of repeating the unnatural frequently enough for your brain to adapt and, slowly, make sustaining love feel almost natural. In the meantime, knowing that sustaining your love is biologically unnatural can allow you to be more forgiving of yourself for the loves you have not sustained.

Sex as Security vs. Sexual Passion

In *Mating In Captivity*, couples therapist Esther Perel articulately shares how the gap between our survival sex role of sex for procreation and our current goal for sex—passion and excitement— are in conflict. Survival sex was all about stability and creating children to enhance survival; sex as passion is ignited by novelty, fantasies of obstacles, pseudodanger, and enhanced desire for a partner at a moment during which they are not easily available.

Everyday life for most couples does not resolve this conflict. Criticism that is repressed undermines both intimacy and passion. Criticism that is expressed to a partner who responds defensively, resulting in a damaging fight, may lead to passionate makeup sex if each partner possesses a strong physical attraction to the other; however, the price is the sacrifice of intimacy and safety.

Role Mate to Soul Mate focuses on two enhancers of sexual passion that *also* enhance stability. First, the Caring and Sharing Practice allows the criticism to be expressed, which stimulates temporary insecurity, and therefore the potential for passion, followed by the criticism being heard, which overcomes the obstacle, often leading to passion. And added to the mix is the listening partner responding with their perspective, which when well heard creates a blend of challenge, respect, and ultimately security with passion.

Second, one of the book's seven secrets is the multiple forms of play—from whimsies to teasing—with the theme that the couple who plays together stays together. We'll see that playing together, including spontaneously dancing together, not only enhances security, but also stimulates passion by breaking the routine and adding an element of surprise and laughter.

Esther Perel describes a problem emanating from an evolutionary shift from survival to fulfillment: the disappointment of an unfulfilled expectation for passion. *Role Mate to Soul Mate* creates a new evolutionary shift—one that shifts our natural defensiveness to criticism to an unnatural association of criticism with an opportunity to be more deeply loved. It is a shift that allows security, intimacy, and passion to coexist. Which is why I encourage couples to reserve a free passion day right after the workshop. Or, as one couple playfully teased, "So the workshop is basically foreplay, eh?"

The Unconditional Love Fallacy

One of the transformations from role mates to soul mates challenges our normal assumptions. We often think of the goal of becoming soul mates is to have unconditional love. No. **Parental love is unconditional. Soulmate love is *more conditional.*** If a woman tells her friend that her husband is emotionally unavailable, won't go to counseling, drinks too much, and that she no longer respects or loves him, her friend may advise, "You don't deserve to be unhappy; you've got to value yourself." Her friend advocates for conditions. The expectation of soul mates is to work on the conditions that deepen their love.

Were our grandparents, with fewer conditions for love, nevertheless happy? Grandma may have felt overwhelmed with raising six children, cooking meals, and cleaning from scratch with neither electronic babysitters nor appliances. However, if she felt respected by her family and friends for supporting her family in these ways, her lower expectations allowed her to consider herself reasonably happy, even though her drinking may have told a different tale. Her goal was not happiness per se. It was surviving and being respected—respected for taking responsibility and fulfilling obligations of her roles: raising children, cooking, and cleaning.

Similarly, although grandpa may have hated his job in the coal mine or returned from war with a lost limb or post-traumatic stress disorder (PTSD), if he felt respected for supporting his family, his lower expectations allowed him to consider himself reasonably happy, even though his drinking may have told an amended tale. His goal was not happiness per se. It was being respected and feeling the self-respect emanating from taking responsibility and fulfilling the obligations necessary to support his family.

This may remind us of Maslow's pyramid showing the hierarchy of needs, with self-actualization at the top of the pyramid.

Maslow's Pyramid of the Hierarchy of Needs

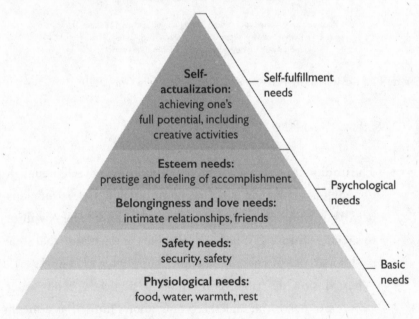

Source: Saul McLeod, Simply Psychology[1]

Now compare Maslow's pyramid to my pyramid of the traditional male hero's values—and see if you can detect its contrast to Maslow's pyramid: compare your observations with my notes below.

Farrell's Hierarchy of the Traditional Male Hero's Values

Safety,
warmth, and rest

Being a dominant,
revered, kind, and wise force

Being a dominant, feared force

Survival (but not safety), food, water

Belongingness and Love Needs: Winning the
hand of a beautiful woman in marriage by protecting and
providing for her and the children

Respect and Approval Needs: Trying to get society's respect
by fulfilling what society expects of him, even if that means being
killed in war or dying from stress from overwork

Source: The Boy Crisis *by Warren Farrell, PhD, and John Gray, PhD*

Note that:

- The traditional male hero is about self-sacrifice, not self-actualization. Self-actualization is not in the traditional male's consciousness. Why? **The more he values himself, the less he is willing to sacrifice himself.** Which explains part of the reason that some traditional male heroes resist couples' communication work.

- What Maslow describes as the most basic needs—food, water, safety—are needs the male hero only allows himself as a means to an end: to have the strength to kill the dragon. Whether he is a marine, Navy SEAL, or firefighter, the hero only allows himself to indulge in safety, warmth, and rest for his own personal comfort *after* his missions are accomplished. Thus, safety, warmth, and rest are missing from the bottom of the hero's pyramid and appear only at the tip of his pyramid, like frosting on the cake of his life.

Similarly, compare Maslow's pyramid with the experience of millions of females in the developed world in the past half century. Their grandmothers felt happy if they had their basic needs met—their survival needs. In the past half century, the women's movement encouraged women to aspire to fulfilling what Maslow calls esteem needs of success both financially and in prestige (e.g., doctor, lawyer, CEO, congresswoman, WNBA star). However, for each woman who made it, many didn't. Their expectations were higher, and they suffered disappointment about something their grandmothers were likely never to have thought of.

With what Maslow calls love needs, as we just saw, more conditions were placed on love and intimate relationships—being role mates and experiencing abuse was not acceptable. What grandma may have accepted as part of "for better or for worse" was now grounds for divorce—or not getting married to begin with. Instead, she may have decided to be a single mom and found herself overwhelmed and dropping her dream of a happy marriage and becoming a doctor.

Unlike grandma, almost every woman in the middle class and above in developed nations in the past half century has been encouraged to find their passion, or what Maslow calls self-actualization: achieving one's full potential, including through creative activities. However, esteem needs are often in conflict with self-actualization. For example, a senior partner of a top corporate law firm likely achieved her esteem needs but rarely feels self-actualized.

And as for what Maslow calls love needs, that female senior partner may feel disappointment at either sacrificing having children or sacrificing time with the children she has—to say nothing of the sacrifice of time with her partner. She may feel angry that, "Unlike men, I can't be a have-it-all woman," but also unlike men, she is more likely to think that being a parent with a man who earns much less but who takes care of the children is marrying down.

These higher expectations create minefields of disappointments that hinder the journey from role mate to soul mate.

One of these minefields—one that is rarely recognized—is the Success-Love Conflict.

The Success-Love Conflict: Why Success at Work Is Often in Conflict with Success in Love

Everyone wishes to minimize their risks of rejection by the people to whom they are most attracted. So we develop a form of "make-up"—what we do to make up the gap between the power we have versus the power we would like to have.

A heterosexual man's make-up may be, for example, to introduce himself as a doctor or colonel—a title he has earned that he feels will likely make a woman feel more receptive to his application for her love.

However, the more a heterosexual woman is comfortable—or even excited—to create her own income, security, and prestigious title, the less she is dependent on this male make-up. She is then freer to feel that any man worth loving will exhibit emotional intelligence and relationship skills. This reasonable expectation is met by an invisible conflict that is therefore never discussed: the Success-Love Conflict.

When a successful woman marries, it is usually to a man who earns as much or more—or is expected to do so soon—as she does. However, the qualities it takes to become successful at work are in tension with the qualities it takes to be successful in love. How?

Imagine a Fortune 50 CEO deciding whether California or Texas is the better location for a massive new project. Perhaps a thousand lobbyists and salespersons with a self-interest in the decision are giving the CEO conflicting advice that they feel would benefit the CEO's company, but more importantly, benefit them.

As each lobbyist or salesperson is selling their product or perspective, it is functional for the CEO to not be solely listening, but to be "self-listening"—to be juggling in her or his mind related factors even as the lobbyist or salesperson is talking. Factors such as the higher California taxes and regulations, whether the best employees could be attracted to sweat out a hot and humid Austin summer, and how the decision would affect the company's reputation and shareholders. The more successful the executive, the more his or her self-listening becomes ingrained and their brain's neuron pathways become hardened.

But when the executive comes home and their spouse, lover, or children share a problem they had at work or school, and the executive self-listens and interrupts with two or three rapid-fire solutions meant to fix the problem, their partner or children feel unheard and unseen and therefore unloved. In this way, **the very qualities that lead to success at work often lead to failure in love.**

In some professions, self-listening is not just likely, but is built in to success. For example, a lawyer who is highly successful is likely to form a rebuttal to what the opposing attorney is saying while the opposing attorney is talking, then interrupt with a distorted version of what the opposing attorney supposedly said—a version that can be more easily rebutted.

To win for a client in court, the highly successful attorney is unlikely to reflexively say what would be functional to win love at home. To win love at home, they might say, with neither sarcasm nor distortion, something like, "What I heard you say is . . ." followed by, with genuine curiosity, "Did I distort anything?" followed by, "Did I miss anything?" followed by, "Is there anything you would like to add?" The attorney would get fired for losing in court with an approach that would win love at home. This is the core of the Success-Love Conflict.

When the successful executive not only self-listens, but also brings work home, whether in their computer or in their mind, and has little time to just hang out with their partner or children, success at work can easily lead to failure in love.

This likelihood is magnified among people who own their own business. **Often business owners aren't sure whether they own their business, or whether their business owns them.**

Understanding the Success-Love Conflict can shift a couple's discussion from more success is better to the trade-offs of success in work and success in love. Being offered a promotion may become less a cause for a family celebration and more a cause for a family discussion. A discussion about what amount of money or success at work is in greatest harmony with the couple's deepening love for each other, their family bonding, and the time they want to spend pursuing what most enriches their life. The family discussion, then, is about the trade-offs of the Success-Love Conflict and the creation of success-love harmony.

Intergenerational Higher Expectations for Role Mate First, Soul Mate Second

Our grandparents' and parents' focus on survival can add to the lack of permission many younger couples feel to focus on fulfillment and love. From our grandparents' perspective, a young father should be adding to both his family's economic security and the nation's GNP. From many young couples' perspective, jobs and careers need to be fulfilling and not create what I call a Father's Catch-22: a dad loving his family by being away from the love of his family.

Marital tension can be created when a young couple perceives their parents or grandparents having little respect for their follow-your-passion aspirations—as if they are defining their GNP as their gross national pleasure. As their parents or grandparents keep pointing out that responsibility includes having enough savings not only to take care of the family they envision, but also to handle economic downturns; loss of jobs; or potential pandemics, medical costs, school costs, and myriad emergencies; the potential dad can feel especially criticized for putting passion before responsibility, and the potential mom can feel criticized for choosing an irresponsible man.

No matter what generation or gender, there is a universal lack of awareness about one thing that has the potential for turning rigid expectations and judgments into a gentler discussion of trade-offs. That one thing is an awareness of exactly how the qualities it takes to become successful at work are often in tension with the qualities it takes to be successful in love.

Progress in Technology Reinforcing our Disappointment in Love

While our relationship communication may be better than that of our grandparents, its failure to keep up with other changes in our lives, such as changes in technology, reinforces our subconscious disappointment. Compare for a moment these advancements in technology just in my lifetime versus the minimal changes in love's "enhancements."

When I was growing up, AI meant artificial insemination. Tik Tok implied a clock. No one did my bidding like Alexa, Siri, or ChatGPT. No one made my deliveries like Amazon. Apple and Blackberry made a fruit salad. A cloud stored rain, not files. A friend was someone who would help me move, not someone whose name I don't recall. Going viral was something I feared, not something I sought. Tweet was the sound of a bird, not a president. Security wasn't cyber. Currency wasn't crypto. And I'd never heard of Microsoft, Facebook, Meta, X, Google, email, iPhone, Bitcoin ... These are just a handful among the hundreds of words symbolizing our changes in technology.

As these enhancements allowed us to worry less about needing love to enhance survival (role-mate marriage), they gave us the freedom to expect love to enhance fulfillment (soul-mate love) and to be disappointed when it didn't.

And our higher expectations have been disappointed. The comparatively minimal progress we have made in relationship skills is reflected by changes in our relationship vocabulary being limited to active listening, emotional intelligence, Mars/Venus differences, and, for perhaps one percent of us, Imago Relationship Therapy.

In brief, we developed sustainable technology before we developed sustainable relationships. *Role Mate to Soul Mate* introduces a practice that incorporates 23 Love Enhancements so we can begin to catch up.

The 23 Soul-Mate Love Enhancements

Some of these enhancements are part of the Seven Secrets (see part II), but most are like Easter eggs hidden in the "lawn" of this book. You will find them hidden where they can be supported by context—by knowing how to apply them.

The 23 Love Enhancements are:

1. The Art and Discipline of Love
2. The Caring and Sharing Practice
3. The Six Mindsets
4. The Caring and Sharing Sandwich
5. 11 Soul-Mate Wisdoms
6. The Power of Wisdom Paradox
7. Panning for the Gold of Appreciating Your Partner
8. Panning for the Gold of Gratitude in Life
9. The Conflict-Free Zone

10. The Love Guarantee

11. Bonding via Playing

12. The "Die-for Mindset"

13. Cinematic Immersion

14. The Four Cs (Depleters of Love)

15. The Four-Part Apology

16. Alone Power

17. The Four Lazinesses

18. Reprogramming Your Home's Feng Shui

19. The "Are-You-OK" Question

20. "Hold"

21. The Aikido Reflex: psychological aikido

22. The Success-Love Conflict

23. Creating Win-Win Solutions to Your Stickiest Problems

It is the practice of integrating these 23 Love Enhancements into a couple's everyday life that creates the outcome of the evolutionary shift from treating perceived criticism as a trigger for defensiveness in preparation for a fight, to a trigger for receptivity in preparation for a deeper love.

Chapter 2

The Four Depleters of Love

*Criticisms, Complaints, Controlling,
and Complacency*

Meditate with me for a minute...

Imagine your partner, let's say in their 30s with no inheritance and no savings, decided that they would not work now or in the future. Nor would they take care of the children. Or shop. Or cook. Or clean up—neither after the family, nor after themself. They would not contribute a cent to the rent or mortgage, nor do a single thing toward the upkeep of the house. They would provide no car and would not offer a dime toward the car's purchase, gas, or maintenance but nevertheless expect you to drive them places. In fact, they would expect you to provide the home, food, and do for them all these things they would not do for you. Oh, and one more thing: they don't want to be prevented from expressing their affections to others besides you.

If such an arrangement was proposed to you, what would be your response? (OK, you have permission to swear [to yourself!], as in "No effing way!") Yet in the US alone, 77 million dogs have an arrangement like this. Not pets, but dogs alone. And at the mere mention of their dog, I have seen many couples' eyes light up—often more than at the mention of their partner. When I discuss this with the couple, their response is usually some version of, "I just feel such *unconditional* love from our dog."

Note that within a few seconds, they've forgotten about all the implicit conditions that they cannot even imagine considering agreeing to with another human, such as only you feed them, clean up their poop, and so on. Even the condition that they be able to express their affections spontaneously to any stranger they want whenever they want!

When I ask in my workshops, "What's going on?" usually someone will volunteer, "When I come home, my dog runs to greet me with these adoring, anticipating eyes. As if I were the most important person in its life."

Ah, now we're beginning to unlock the secret of what the dog offers: the feeling of being so loved and so important. Feeling loved and important is so empowering that we become literally unconscious of the conditions.

A man in a workshop elaborated on this: "In my previous marriage, I felt like I was way down the line of importance to my wife: after our three children, which I understood; after her career, which I was proud of. But after her yoga practice, after her weekend hikes, after her best friend, after long calls with her mom, and, oh yes, definitely after the dog, and then, *maybe*, there was me. There was virtually no physical affection, not even mercy sex. And maybe worst of all, I didn't feel respected.

"In contrast, when I come home and our dog runs to the door the second I approach, it feels like he's been waiting for me—and only me—all day. During those few minutes, I no longer feel like leftovers."

Well, that is what the dog gives us. Just as important is what the dog does not give us: **criticism**. In fact, the dog does not give us *any* of the Four Cs.

What the Four Cs Would Be Like
If They Came from Your Dog

1. **Criticisms:** "Why do you just stroke me on my neck?"
2. **Complaints:** "What? *I* give *you* a feeling of being all-important, and *you* just give *me* dog food?"
3. **Control:** "The dinner on your plate is mine. Either hand it over, or I'll jump on the table and take it."
4. **Complacency:** "Next time you come home, I yawn."

The human versions of the Four Cs manifest a bit differently. Fortunately, I incorporate solutions to each, which can even turn some of these depleters of love into ways of deepening love. That's especially true of criticisms and complaints, each of which serve an important function in helping us express the challenges we feel that if not heard would inhibit a deeper love.

The Four Cs Human-Style

Criticism

We've already seen how the Achilles' heel of humans, our inability to hear personal criticism from a loved one without becoming defensive, likely evolved from criticism often coming from a potential enemy, and survival being enhanced by a rapid response in defense.

Ironically, the more we love our partner, the more vulnerable we feel, so the more defensive we become. Intellectual insights from couples' books or courses disappear when criticism appears. That is, when criticism appears, wisdom disappears.

Learning how to substitute this natural response of defensiveness with the unnatural response of associating criticism with an opportunity to be more deeply loved is an in-depth process that I call the Caring and Sharing

Practice. I describe it step-by-step in chapter 6. Before we get to the practice, the first challenge of making this evolutionary shift is understanding the perception gap between the alleged criticizer and the criticized.

- **The Criticizer:** The criticizer often feels they are not criticizing their partner but merely sharing a concern or suggesting a change to improve the situation, usually intended to *increase* intimacy.
- **The Criticized:** The person hearing their loved one make any suggestion for a change in attitude or behavior often experiences it as criticism. They experience a *decrease* in intimacy.

Here are two real-life examples from my retreats and home coaching.

Sandy, who had flown into California from North Carolina with her husband, shared this example. "Our daughter lives in the San Fransisco Bay Area, and she attended your workshop a couple of years ago after she and her husband had kids and began to run into problems. Then, as our 30th anniversary approached, they gave us this workshop as a gift.

"When Bill and I got married, our relationship was filled with passion. I had watched him play basketball when we were both attending Duke and couldn't believe it when he took an interest in me. Unfortunately, Bill recently had an affair that I discovered when he had misplaced his iPhone. I found it and saw some messages that, well, were a giveaway. When I confronted him, he eventually acknowledged it and said it was because our marriage had become sexless, and he knew that any initiative he took with me would just lead to rejection.

"I knew that was true. When he sentimentally recalled that I used to be so attracted to him, and how he loved how I sometimes even initiated sex after we were married, he asked what happened?" I brought up the impact of having children, exhaustion, and so on. But I hesitated to add another reason.

"When I saw his eyes searching, as if to say, 'I can't change the impact of the children, but is there anything I can do?' it encouraged me to be honest.

"Then it all poured out, maybe a bit to hurt him back like I'd been hurt, but anyway I said something like, 'Bill, we've both gained weight since our college days, but you've gained a lot of weight, and especially I get, well, turned off by your sagging belly. And when you eat a lot of greasy, fatty fries while downing beer, it makes me feel you don't care—about yourself or me. I guess it makes me lose respect for you.'"

I asked Sandy, "What was your best intent in sharing this?"

"To give Bill something he could do that was in his control that would make me feel both more respect for him, and maybe reignite my physical attraction and sexual interest."

"And, Bill, how did you feel after Sandy shared this?"

"Awful. I felt she didn't have to say the stuff about losing respect for me. That cut me to the core. Even if she had expressed some sexual interest after that, I don't know that I'd be able to respond."

"That's why we're here," Sandy offered. "The Caring and Sharing process is the first time that we've both fully heard each other. Warren, I think we're ready for the next part—where we create win-win solutions."

I didn't get to hear how Sandy and Bill's solutions worked until a follow-up call about six months later.

Sandy began, "It took our feelings to be heard before we could work on the solutions. We both committed to four things: going to Weight Watchers, Bill committing to exercise, me committing to setting aside intimacy time each week, and Bill giving up his affair."

Bill added, "I organized a bunch of guys to play basketball, not just half court, but full court, and the combination of that and Weight Watchers has led to my losing almost 20 pounds and feeling a lot better. My goal is to lose another 10 pounds. And, yes, I gave up the affair and feel like Sandy and I have found some passion again."

Sandy added, " My respect for him definitely increased—and, yes, the other thing increased too!"

In brief, Sandy and Bill used two processes to make the transition from feeling hurt and disrespected to feeling reconnected with the underlying problems resolved: the two secrets called the Caring and Sharing Practice (chapter 6) and Creating Win-Win Solutions (chapter 10).

Improving or Criticizing?

When I introduced the criticizer/criticized perception gap in relation to improving a situation, Mary volunteered, "Joan and I both teach and have had a wonderful last ten summers and holidays traveling the world. Well, a few months ago we were preparing for a party. I dug out of the closet some of my favorite dishes from our travels, washed them off, and set them out on the table very aesthetically. Then I went to take a shower and change for the party.

"When I returned, I immediately noticed that Joan had replaced some dishes with others, and altered the location of many of the remaining dishes. I definitely experienced that as criticism. And Joan didn't say anything. Which I felt was pretty sneaky, and maybe passive-aggressive."

Joan added, "I told Mary that I felt I was adding my touch to her touch and showing her that I also care about the aesthetics, which she often criticizes me for not caring enough about. And I explained that I didn't say anything not out of sneakiness but because I didn't want to toot my own horn, or call attention to my little contribution."

In this case, not a word of criticism was spoken. What Joan experienced as adding a contribution to Mary's, Mary experienced as a criticism of her contribution.

Complaining

As with criticism, there is often a perception gap between the complainer and the listening partner:

- **The Complainer:** The complainer usually feels they are only complaining about the situation (e.g., the restaurant or movie).
- **The Listening Partner:** If the listening partner feels they had anything to do with creating that situation, they often experience the complaint as being about them.

I witnessed an example of this complaining gap with a couple coming to my home for the "Role Mate to Soul Mate" course. When they returned on Saturday morning, I felt some tension.

"I sense a little mood change. What's up?"

Andy began, "As you know, last night was our fifth anniversary. So I had researched the best restaurant in this area and found that El Paseo here in Mill Valley had a Michelin one star rating and was owned by Tyler Florence, who Megan had loved after seeing him on TV. So I surprised her and made reservations there.

"Well, we both loved the brick and rustic interior, but when the soup came, Megan mentioned that it was bland. When dinner was served, she complained that the salmon was too rare. I tried not to take either comment personally, but when she said how aloof the server was, and then commented that her spicy margarita wasn't very spicy, I felt like a total failure.

"I said, 'You're such a complainer.' Megan was offended and shot back something like, 'I feel I can't express my feelings and just be honest with you. Don't you agree? Didn't you think the waiter was inattentive?'"

I asked Megan to reverse roles—to pretend she had researched for the best restaurant and one owned by a chef that Andy revered and took care of making a reservation there for your anniversary.

Megan softened and responded with empathy. "I was complaining about the restaurant, not you. But I can see how, if I had made all that effort to choose a restaurant that would make you happy on our anniversary, one owned by a favorite chef of yours, and all I heard from you were complaints about the soup, the service, the salmon, and your margarita. it would make me feel that I had failed."

Megan and Andy hugged.

When I told Andy and Megan that Tyler Florence had just moved and given up the restaurant, we all had a big laugh!

An Exercise

Take a moment to recall any complaints you have made about not only restaurants, but also movie recommendations, past vacation selections that your partner had taken primary responsibility for recommending, or complaints about a person your partner had researched and recommended for interior design, landscaping, or construction. Write them down.

Is the solution to shut up about anything your partner had a role in selecting with which you find a problem? No. Feedback is essential to growing our love. But before you complain, try this:

Now that you know that a complaint about something recommended by your loved one might be perceived as a complaint about them, consider the reverse, that a compliment about their recommendation will likely be experienced as a compliment about them.

Some possibilities:

1. "I love the softness of the lighting in here—it's so romantic; perfect for our anniversary. It brings back romantic memories from the restaurant we went to on our first date."

2. "I love the brick on the walls. It's so rich and rustic. It makes me feel like we're in the mountains."

3. "I like that they have carpeting on the floor. It absorbs the noise of other people talking so I can hear you better."

4. "I like the design on the carpet—do you?"

5. "Don't you think that soft white tablecloths like these create such a feeling of luxury?"

6. "I like that their napkins don't leave lint on our clothes."

7. "I appreciate we came here early so it isn't too crowded, and we can easily hear each other."

8. "Oh, look at this. They have Wagyu steak on the menu. I'm going to order that."

9. "I like that you chose a restaurant near a wooded area so we can take an after-dinner stroll. Did you have that in mind?"

Seven of these nine examples could easily have been observed about El Paseo—even after Tyler Florence had left!

Recall that this takes the discipline of consciously making yourself aware not only of everything you like about the restaurant, vacation, interior designer, or movie (after it ends!), but also why.

When you believe there is even a chance that your partner may have had what you appreciate in mind when they made their recommendation, then add that to your appreciation. (If you're wrong, not to worry. They'll either take the undeserved compliment with pleasure, or feel virtuous for telling you they don't deserve it. And who knows, it may give your partner a hint about what might be considered in his or her next recommendation!)

Remember this exercise. We'll see why it works so well in the chapter on appreciations, chapter 5, "Secret 1."

Controlling
An Exercise

Ask yourself:

"Do I criticize my partner more than I feel is optimal?"

"Do I complain about something my partner recommended more than I feel is optimal?"

The majority of people in my workshops answer yes to the questions about whether they criticize and complain more than is optimal. But when I ask them if they feel they are controlling, most say no.

Now complete the exercise by answering this question:

"When my partner criticizes me a lot, and frequently complains about my recommendations, do I sometimes feel controlled?"

Most participants say that they would feel controlled by a partner who is often criticizing them and complaining about their recommendations, which gives them an understanding of how their loved one may experience them as controlling. If we can understand that we feel controlled when our loved one criticizes us and complains about what we take responsibility for, that's a good start toward stopping two behaviors that lead our partner to experience us as controlling.

The good news is that most of us are willing and able to criticize and complain less—two solutions to being controlling.

Complacency

I begin each workshop by playing Barbra Streisand and Neil Diamond's rendition of "You Don't Bring Me Flowers." It represents all too poignantly most couples' transition from passion to complacency—the last of the Four Cs.

The transition to complacency is ubiquitous. We carefully selected what we wore for our first date. But now we wear baggy sweatpants around the house without even saying "around our partner." Yet when we're dressing for a party, we change out of the baggy sweatpants and check with our partner about what looks best on us for *others* to see!

During our first passionate encounters, we took care not to pick our nose, burp, fart, swear, or talk with our mouth full. Now they're all on display on our journey to complacency.

Complacency creates a transition from excitement about seeing our partner to fantasies of passion with new partners, and sometimes to affairs and either "minimum-security-prison marriages" or divorce. Complacency does have an upside. We replace the passion of specialness with comfort. The comfort of knowing we're accepted as we are.

Oh yes, and there's another benefit to complacency. In the US complacency opens the door for 77 million dogs to get their room, board, and poop picked up in exchange for filling our specialness void!

An Exercise: The ABCs (attitudes, behaviors, and clothes) of Complacency

Do not share your answers to the four questions below until you schedule a special Caring and Sharing session about complacency.

1. Write down six things you do around your partner that you wouldn't do at a party (e.g., wear a ragged shirt or baggy pants, burp, or pick your nose).
2. Write down three things you could do differently around your

partner that would show less complacency while not sacrificing too much comfort.

3. Write down six things your partner does that make them less attractive to you.

4. Write down three things your partner could do differently to make them more attractive to you.

The solution to these Four Cs? Each of the 23 Love Enhancements contributes to ways of transforming the Four Depleters of Love into a deepening of love. Let's start with some soul-mate wisdoms.

Chapter 3

Soul-Mate Wisdoms

These Soul-Mate Wisdoms can either be quickly read and quickly forgotten, or repeatedly reviewed and slowly woven in to your natural way of responding, or your foundational wisdom. When you and your partner have both strengthened your foundational wisdom, it also becomes your soul-mate wisdom. There's one problem. That criticism devil. Wisdom #11 below gives you two practices to dilute criticism's power.

With many of these wisdoms I indicate where they are discussed in greater depth. This chapter gives a quick overview to encourage repeated reviews.

Soul-Mate Wisdom 1: The secret to feeling loved is feeling understood; no one says, "I want a divorce, my partner understand me"

Millions of women with beautiful diamonds are nevertheless filing for divorce. Few, if any of them, feel understood.

Among men, sex workers report that many men seem to care more about being understood than actual physical intimacy.

In Japan, an institution known as the snack is used by men to stop on the way home from work to order a snack for which he pays significantly more than he otherwise would. What's the appeal? The female server spends time listening to him while he shares his disappointments, accomplishments, feelings, and fears—to understand him. (Note there is no sex, just listening. There may not even be empathy, just listening, just feeling heard, which is usually enough to make us feel understood.) In this way, he doesn't lose face with his wife or make her worry that her provider/protector has fears that might undermine his ability to provide and protect.

Among same-sex couples in my workshops, the primary yearning is the same: the deep desire to be heard, seen, and understood.

Neither diamonds nor sex fill the unheard heart.

Soul-Mate Wisdom 2: Our choice of partner is the most important statement about our choice of values

Before you criticize your partner, take responsibility for what motivated your choice.

I sometimes half joke, "Opposites attract; they just can't live together." Whether in marriage or in a long-term relationship, we often choose someone who is the opposite of ourselves because they contribute something we are missing. The spiritual, spontaneous, new age artist or writer needs the logical scientist or executive for financial support. Conversely, the logical financial supporter feels enlivened by the spontaneous soul.

Trouble begins as the financial supporter begins to lose respect for what he or she considers the spontaneous soul's lack of financial responsibility or maturity. Conversely, the spontaneous soul begins to feel a diminished love for the financial supporter's lack of spontaneity, emotional intelligence, or interest in personal growth as manifested by a reluctance to enroll in a yoga class or go to a "Role Mate to Soul Mate" workshop. And as we saw with the Success-Love Conflict (chapter 1), the qualities it takes to be highly successful in work are often in tension with the qualities it takes to be successful in love.

Part of the problem is that neither the financially successful person nor the spontaneous soul is taking responsibility for their role in enabling the other to be what they are now criticizing. The artist would have to figure out a way to create income if the income disappeared; the financial supporter would feel less pressure to produce money if someone were helping more with the income so they would have more time for yoga class.

The wisdom? Our choice of partner is our most important single statement about our choice of values. Before you blame your partner, look in the mirror for five things:

1. Whether your choice of partner was in part about what you were missing in yourself
2. Whether you are blaming your partner for being what you chose
3. Whether you are enabling your partner to be what you are complaining about
4. Whether your choice of partner reflects your choice of values
5. Whether your partner feels they need to remain the way they are to remain attractive to you

Soul-Mate Wisdom 3: Every virtue taken to its extreme becomes a vice

The ability of our virtues to attract love, praise, and pay often seduces us into magnifying our virtues to the extreme while being blinded to the degree those virtues are morphing into vices. Examples:

1. Makeup covers our flaws, but we may use so much of it that makeup becomes a flaw.
2. A parent is so devoted to their children that the children feel the world is centered on them.
3. A cardiac surgeon is devoted to their specialty but leaves their family feeling neglected.

How does this happen? Well, would you rather have a cardiac surgeon who is devoted to their specialty or one who is devoted to their family? We benefit more from the specialist, which tempts the specialist to hone the virtue of specializing at work and develop the vice of neglecting family at home.

Soul-Mate Wisdom 4: Criticism looks different to the criticizer and the criticized

We did a deep dive into this wisdom in chapter 2, "The Four Depleters of Love." Remember:

- **The Criticizer:** The criticizer often feels they are not criticizing their partner but merely sharing a concern or suggesting a change to improve the situation, usually intended to *increase* intimacy.
- **The Criticized:** The person hearing their loved one make any suggestion for a change in attitude or behavior often experiences it as criticism. They experience a *decrease* in intimacy.

Soul-Mate Wisdom 5: Anger is vulnerability's mask

Whenever you see anger, think vulnerability.

When we see only the anger, we respond to that anger with anger.

When we see the vulnerability, we can respond to the vulnerability with empathy.

Is it true, though, that anger is vulnerability's mask? Check it out. Which makes you feel more vulnerable? Being distorted and interrupted by someone you love *or* by someone you just met on a plane? Is it what also makes you angrier?

Recall a great first date. You told your friends it was a perfect match. But then the person neither called you nor called you back. On the flip-side, consider a bad first date. You hoped the person would never call again, and, in fact, they never did.

If the potential perfect match neither called nor called back, you might have labeled them a jerk to your friends. Why? It hurts less to be rejected by an object (a jerk) than by a human being. Your anger ("What a jerk!") was an effort to reduce your vulnerability. As for that *bad* first date, where there's no vulnerability, there's no anger.

Anger as vulnerability's mask is especially apparent after divorce. Divorce often generates four vulnerabilities:

1. The vulnerability of love
2. Demolished expectations ('til death do us part)
3. Internal feelings of self-judgment as a failure
4. Fear of external judgment as being a failure by family and friends (often, the bigger the wedding, the greater the vulnerability/anger)

If the vulnerability is enormous, the anger is enormous.

When your loved one is angry, they almost invariably desire to feel your empathy for their vulnerability, not your anger at their anger. Your empathy—and only your empathy—can reduce your partner's anger.

The anger-is-vulnerability's-mask wisdom, then, is a two-way street:

- When your loved one is angry, search for the vulnerability.
- When you are expressing anger, search for and then express your vulnerability.

Soul-Mate Wisdom 6: Falling in love is biologically natural; sustaining love is biologically unnatural

Yes, this again! Since the unnatural practice of sustaining love is *Role Mate to Soul Mate's* core practice, it deserves its place among the foundational wisdoms. For a deep dive, see the entire book!

Soul-Mate Wisdom 7: The path to relationship wealth is appreciating your partner as if you are panning for gold

The path to relationship wealth involves ignoring our loved one's "little stones" and panning for our loved one's "gold." The path to relationship poverty involves walking over our partner's gold without noticing it. The path to the end of a relationship is both focusing on the little stones and ignoring the gold.

The secret sauce of relationship wealth is both appreciating our partner and making our appreciations specific. Specific appreciations fill our reservoir of love. If our reservoir of love is empty, there is no incentive to discipline oneself to sustain an empty reservoir. That's why mastering the art and discipline of specific appreciations is the first of the seven secrets (chapter 5).

Soul-Mate Wisdom 8: The more you love your partner, the more vulnerable you feel, so the harder it is to hear your partner's criticism without reflexively defending yourself.

If you and your partner are predictably defensive in response to perceived criticism, rather than interpret it as "we're hopeless, we'll be better off apart," consider the possibility that your vulnerability reflects the depth of your love, as does your defensiveness. (See Wisdom 5, "Anger is vulnerability's mask.")

Soul-Mate Wisdom 9: When either of us wins, both of us lose

I occasionally hear someone boast, "I won that argument." You can rest assured: if you think you've won, you've lost. You've both lost. **Solving arguments with arguments does not solve arguments.**

Soul-Mate Wisdom 10: Never say what you don't want; *ask* for what you *do* want

How? (See chapter 8, "Secret 4: The Magic of the Ask.")

Soul-Mate Wisdom 11: When criticism appears, wisdom disappears

The above wisdoms can create your foundational relationship wisdom. The problem is that when the earthquake called criticism appears, your foundational wisdom may disappear. This is **The Power of Wisdom Paradox: these wisdoms offer both the power of wisdom and the limitation of wisdom's power.** Fortunately, the following two practices taken together will circumvent the limitation:

First, review these wisdoms frequently enough for your neurons to fire and your foundational wisdom to be strengthened.

Second, practice the Caring and Sharing time consistently for between a few months and a year.

When practiced together, the foundational wisdom responds to criticism like a strong foundation responds to an earthquake—with minimal damage and faster reconstruction.

———

After you and your partner have reviewed the Soul-Mate Wisdoms, tell each other which three you would most like to incorporate into your body of wisdom. Consider incorporating these into your closing ceremony involving your commitments to change and your renewal of vows (see chapter 13).

Chapter 4

Exploring the Nature of Your Love and the Style of Your Defensiveness

Prior to exploring the seven secrets to a deeper love, let's take a look at the nature of your love and identify your particular style of defensiveness—the most important single barrier.

Exploring the Nature of Your Love

Write out the four questions below on a notepad. Then sit across from your partner facing each other and looking into each other's eyes. One of you begins by reading the questions aloud, then sharing your answers with your partner. Then reverse the process. The listening partner just listens—no interruptions, no commentary.

---

1. **What made you fall in love?**
   This may be the initial hit of chemistry when you first met or the first time you felt you loved your partner. Or some combination.
2. **What is your partner's biggest challenge with you?**
   Your best guess. No input or response from partner.
3. **What's your biggest challenge with your partner?**
   No discussion.
4. **What do you most appreciate about your partner?**

When you've both finished, discuss your answers to each of these questions. If your partner doesn't feel you've accurately identified their biggest challenge with you, just listen to their perspective.

Identifying Your Style of Defensiveness

We hone defenses based on a lifetime of experience as to what has worked best for us to either avoid blame or minimize its consequences. We then adapt to what works best with our present partner. For example, if we're a good debater, we may have honed the art of self-listening: planning our response as our partner is criticizing us. If we know our partner is a better debater or gets upset or withdraws emotionally and sexually when we disagree, we may adapt and begin to hone the art of passive-aggressiveness.

Since our defenses prevent our partner from being heard, and therefore feeling loved—and a person who doesn't feel loved *by* you can't really love you—becoming conscious of your style of defensiveness is a first step toward identifying what you need to work on to deepen your love.

Start by filling out the following questionnaire. If you need one for each of you, you can print them out from the handouts that accompany the online "Role Mate to Soul Mate" course (see Appendix).

On the questionnaire, check the answer you are most likely to give when you are in the process of being bombarded by anger or criticism, not the answer that when your intellect walks back into your brain (!) you wish you had given. Don't let yourself get bogged down with "Well, it depends." Just check what you most often do before you think it through. (Note, the (c) option is just my sense of humor.)

Questionnaire on Your Style of Defensiveness

Say this before each multiple-choice question: "When my partner criticizes me or gets angry, I am more likely to . . ."

1. __ (a) point out my partner's equivalent shortcomings ("Well, you often interrupt me")
   __ (b) share with my partner what I heard them say with empathy in my eyes, love in my voice, and all that positive attitude stuff
   __ (c) ... I chose (*b*), but I'm in denial.

2. __ (a) criticize my partner's **style** (e.g., "The sarcasm in your voice made me tune out," "You *always* exaggerate")
   __ (b) look beyond the style to my partner's best intent
   __ (c) ... I chose (*b*), but I'm in denial.

3. __ (a) criticize my partner's **demeanor** (e.g., "You look so angry, it scares me," "You're hypersensitive")
   __ (b) be compassionate no matter what my partner's demeanor is
   __ (c) ... I chose (*b*), but I'm in denial.

4. __(a)   look for the **flaw** in the accuracy of the criticism
   __(b)   look for the germ of truth

5. __(a)   distort what my partner said until I create something I
            can effectively debate
   __(b)   search for my partner's most valid point and acknowledge
            it

6. __(a)   sidestep my partner's deepest underlying concern and
            while my partner's blabbing on figure out what I have
            the best response to and focus on that
   __(b)   deal directly with my partner's deepest concern, even if it
            puts me in a bad light

7. __(a)   feel impatient (as in "I know what you mean. Shut up
            already")
   __(b)   be genuinely patient out of an understanding that the
            more your partner feels it's safe to express negative feel-
            ings to you, the closer they will feel to you

8. __(a)   say some version of "If you really feel that way, then it's
            hopeless"
   __(b)   say some version of "Your willingness to express feelings
            gives me more hope for intimacy"

9. __(a)   wait for my partner to apologize first
   __(b)   apologize first

10. __(a   hold a grudge
    __(b) let it go

11. __(a) emotionally withdraw

  __(b) become more caring

12. __(a) sexually withdraw

  __(b) sexually open up

When finished, exchange questionnaires, then each of you write #1 by the defense that most bothers you about your partner, and #2 by the defense that is the second-most bothersome. Now return the question-naire to your partner.

The purpose of identifying your particular style of defensiveness is to bring it to the conscious level so you can eliminate not just that particular style of defensiveness but *your defensiveness completely* in response to your partner's expression of feelings.

Keep this questionnaire until you have completed the book. Then during the closing ceremony, if you feel you have been able to eliminate your defenses, you can participate in the ritual of ripping up your ques-tionnaire as a symbolic gesture of your commitment to "rip up" your defenses.

PART II

THE SEVEN SECRETS TO A DEEPER LOVE

Chapter 5

Secret 1: Appreciations and Gratitude

Panning for Your Partner's Gold, and Panning for the Gold in Life

"I can live for two months on a good compliment."

Mark Twain

We explored in chapter 2, "The Four Depleters of Love," exactly how criticism and complacency drain the reservoir of love, and we began to look at how appreciation can fill it. As we've seen, many humans would do more for their dog than their human partner in part because they feel so appreciated and desired by their dog. And now the dog has a competitor who also expresses love and appreciation for you and who also doesn't criticize you or become complacent. And unlike dogs, they don't poop or expect you to feed them the latest human-grade dog food.

Doggies are so upset with this low expectation, cheap competitor

that they are forming an IDU (an international doggie union, of course!).
What could be threatening the livelihood of man's best friend? Answer:
a woman's best friend *and* a man's best friend—or everyone's BFF: emotional support chatbots. Companies such as Replika and Inflection AI,
the manufacturer of emotional support chatbot Pi, are programming
chatbots to hear what is bothering you, give you soothing and supportive
answers, and express constant appreciation for you.

What both dogs and emotional support chatbots tell us is how important it is to feel supported and appreciated without being criticized or
feeling complacency set in.

Fortunately, humans who know how to appreciate and overcome the
other obstacles to deeper love can give our loved one virtually everything
the dog offers and then some. We can bear and raise children and grand-
children, be partners in life's decisions, help produce income, share responsibilities such as running errands and providing childcare, do Caring
and Sharing sessions, make love, and be attentive to each other's health.

For now, though, with the inspiration of our dogs, let's begin developing the art and discipline of appreciation soul mate–style. Let's start by
taking inventory.

Appreciation Exercise: Taking Inventory

1. Write down every appreciation you have given your partner either verbally or in writing in the past seven days that you are
   quite sure your partner will recall. If there are none, not to
   worry—that's the norm. And this chapter will help you deepen
   your love even more.
2. If you have written down any appreciations, show them to your
   partner. If your partner does not recall one or more of them,
   don't argue about it. We'll explore many ways you can make
   your appreciations more frequent and more memorable.

Sustaining Love's First Step: Filling the Reservoir of Love

There's little incentive to do the hard work of sustaining love if the reservoir of love is depleted. The best way to refill the reservoir is by mastering both the art and discipline of appreciating your partner.

Appreciations are a form of intentional romance. They are ways of giving your partner an opportunity to be a hero to you in the future rather than being a failure to you in the past.

Finding appreciations is like panning for gold. The people who got rich during the gold rush didn't get rich by focusing on the stones and clay. The path to relationship poverty involves walking over our partner's gold without noticing it. The path to relationship wealth involves developing a keen eye for our partner's "gold."

The *Art* of Appreciation

The art of appreciation includes making the content creative and then expressing it creatively. You can express your appreciation via voicemail, email, Post-it, text, or finger writing through the steam on your bathroom mirror after you shower.

Creative Appreciations: Four Examples

1. The Anxiety-Relief Bonding Enhancer

Say you're on vacation. Your partner drove through a beautiful mountain area with each curve in the road exposing yet another unique view. Later that evening, you tuck a faux ticket under the windshield wiper. Relieved it's not a ticket, your partner reads, "Thank you for making the drive safe so I could absorb the beauty of our trip."

49

Let's deconstruct this form of creativity.

The two or three seconds of anxiety your partner experienced before the "ticket" was re-experienced as an appreciation, enhancing the *memorability* of the experience. The shared moment of anxiety, humor, and playfulness is usually a *bonding* experience. Of course, the second or two of anxiety is a virtue that, taken to the extreme, becomes a vice.

Part of bonding is deepening your understanding of what type of playfulness works with your partner and what circumstances and mood are optimal. That is, discovering what's a virtue and what's a vice for your unique personalities in partnership at any given point in time.

Your bonding as a couple is deepened as you laugh with friends over stories like this. Especially if there's a mishap. Great stories often emanate from mishaps; they rarely emanate from the mundane.

Once you've used the ticket experience, you might play with, for example, an email whose subject line is "Urgent Notice, Fine, or Overdue Bill."

2. Self-Deprecating Humor with Apology

Imagine that during that same vacation mountain drive you had repeatedly warned your partner "Be careful. That's a sharp curve." Your faux ticket might read, "We're a great team: you drive me through the mountains; I drive you crazy." An apology with a little self-deprecating humor can be to your partner what a charging station is to an EV running low on electricity.

3. Snowflakes of Love

A man in one of my workshops wrote an appreciation of about 15 words on white paper. He cut it into 15 pieces and carefully placed the pieces on top of the door to the bedroom. When his wife opened the door, the papers flittered to the floor like snowflakes.

Her "job" was to piece the words together until she could read the full appreciation. The outcome? Well, he denied to the workshop that he consciously planned it as the best foreplay he and his wife had experienced in years!

This appreciation had many of the ingredients we discussed above: memorability; a great future story that also recalls some precious moments and creative thoughtfulness; and bonding on both the emotional and ultimately physical level.

4. My Heart, Your Heart

Be inspired by the true-to-life heart created by Annie, which she demonstrates in the "Role Mate to Soul Mate" online course. (See final page for QR code.) As she holds it up with a little key next to the heart, she tells her partner, Eben, "My heart feels the safest when it is beside your heart. Here's a little key to my heart. There's only one, and you have it."

Carpe Diem Appreciations

Panning for gold includes panning for situations that will allow you to seize the opportunity with a carpe diem appreciation. For example:

1. **Leftovers:** Your partner cooked a great dinner or made an excellent salad. You put a Post-it with a note about how much you enjoyed it front and center in the fridge on your favorite leftover, so when your partner next opens the fridge, your appreciation of what your partner made can't be missed.

2. **No Leftovers:** Put a Post-it on an empty container that might read, "Thank you for a dinner so yummy it filled my tummy and left this container empty!"

3. **Partner Worked Late:** Rather than focusing on the disappointment, you pan for gold with a creative appreciation such as a poem, on the fridge by a welcome-home drink or on a pillow.

And If You're Not a Good Poet: Write a simple poem. Simple poems are remembered longer. Ogden Nash used to lament that despite all his sophisticated poetry, he was remembered most for one line: "Candy is dandy, but liquor is quicker." A simple poem is often received more purely by the heart than a sophisticated poem. Think of how we would respond more to something written by a child than by an adult. So try a simple poem like:

Thanks for working hard
To make the dime
So I can recover
With more relax time

———

The #1 Secret Sauce of Appreciation: Specificity

The more specific an appreciation, the more it is appreciated. Here are two specificity blends:

1. Specificity with a Touch of Curiosity

When you tell your partner, "You're a good cook," you'll probably hear, "Thank you." But each level of specificity, especially when a touch of curiosity is mixed in, allows your partner to feel more seen and respected by you, or, in the example that follows, perhaps by both you and your guests. For example:

Level 1: You're a good cook.

Level 2: I liked the way you cooked the turkey.

Level 3: How did you get the skin so crisp?

Level 4: How did you get the dressing to such a perfect level of moisture?

Level 5: I loved the cranberries, grapes, and spices and herbs.

Level 6: Did you use parsley, sage, rosemary, thyme, or anything else from Simon and Garfunkle?

Level 7: May I have the recipe?

2. Specificity with a Guess as to Best Intent

Specificity might also be combined with a leap of faith that anything that coincides with one of your preferences was intentional (as in levels 3–6):

Level 1: Thank you for bringing me flowers.

Level 2: Thank you for bringing me flowers even though it *wasn't* a special occasion. It makes me feel like *I* am your special occasion.

Level 3: Thank you for bringing me begonias, remembering that begonias are my favorite flower.

Level 4: Thank you for bringing me apricot begonias. I love that you remember apricot is my favorite color.

Level 5: Thank you for bringing me tuberous begonias, recalling they are my favorite type of begonia since we have the morning sun that begonias love.

Level 6: Thank you for bringing me potted begonias, remembering that I love to plant the begonias in the garden rather than watch them quickly die.

Specific and Creative Appreciations Exercise

Using a notebook with lines, write down:

1. Ten new appreciations of your partner, with five empty lines following each appreciation.
2. For just four of the ten appreciations (we'll get to more later), write five or six levels of specificity in the empty lines. Add the spice of curiosity.
3. Choose from among those four specific appreciations just **one** that you feel you can best develop as a **creative** appreciation. (Recall the white papers falling from the top of the door like snowflakes, or the simple poems.) Share that creative appreciation that night or the following day.
4. Choose **two** of the three remaining appreciations to share with each other *now*. (Don't share the creative appreciation now—save that as a surprise.) Sit across from each other. Choose one partner to do both appreciations first.

Coming up with these multiple levels of specificity takes us out of our comfort zone of giving a general appreciation. It requires both art and discipline.

The *Discipline* of Appreciating

To mentally search for every aspect of what someone does that might be appreciated takes considerable discipline. And it sometimes takes a leap of faith to assert that anything that is congruent with what you like was in fact *intended* to please you. You might even feel it is a bit disingenuous to give credit where credit may not be due. Well, I'll address that with a simple poem:

Worried about giving credit
Where credit isn't due?
Your loved one will love it
So should you!

While giving specific appreciations requires discipline, if appreciations are rarely given, the discipline of being specific is worth little.

The discipline of appreciating involves two additional parts:

1. **Establishing a routine with frequency:** Set aside about 15 minutes one day each week to share three specific appreciations with your partner. For example, it might be each Wednesday night at dinner. Place a reminder notification on your computer to keep alerting you each week on that day. If you have children, include them. You may wish to do this either in conjunction with family dinner night or separately. In either case, if your children can be included, first read chapter 11, "Creating Family Dinner Nights So They Don't Become Family Dinner Nightmares." Similarly, you might make appreciations a routine part of your family's auto trip.

   One warning about teaching your children the art and discipline of appreciating others: they may become the most popular kids in school! (Which is one of those virtues that, if taken to an extreme, can become a vice.)

2. **Share appreciations spontaneously throughout the week:** Combine the discipline of panning for gold with spontaneously sharing any appreciation your panning reveals. (I sometimes tell Liz "I love you" when she's asleep. Once she caught me!)

———

Gratitude: Panning for the Gold in Life

While specific appreciations are soul-mate enhancing, the art and discipline of being specific about what we have to be grateful for in life is, well, life enhancing.

Studies are increasingly showing that gratitude may, for example, benefit our cardiovascular health, reduce inflammation, improve the quality of our sleep, and decrease stress. And a review of 70 studies finds that more gratitude is associated with less depression.[2]

With that in mind, Liz and I have added a different type of appreciation to our lives: a gratitude evening. For example, as we're getting older, we could complain that we're taking many more supplements and seeing doctors a lot more often. And yes, we do complain about both of those! But for our gratitude evening, we focus on our good health and that part of the reason we are in good health is due to those supplements (probably), good doctors, the availability of organic food, and the option of having healthy food delivered to us or going to a restaurant should we be too tired to cook.

Similarly, we could get down on ourselves for still working close to full time at well past retirement age or for feeling more exhausted after a full day's work than we were 40 years ago. For our gratitude evenings, though, the focus is on the gratitude we feel for having found work that excites us and gives us a sense of purpose, being our own bosses, and being able to work out of our home where we can have contact with each other. We may also focus on knowing that we can, should we wish, stop working at any time (or laugh at ourselves for having what I call "work-*work* balance").

The gratitude evening may morph into showing appreciation for each other. For instance, for encouraging each other to see a doctor that we might not otherwise have done because we were too busy with our work.

But for the gratitude evening, we start with an appreciation of our situation, not each other.

The gratitude evenings are an important balance to the propensity people have to focus on fears. This focus on fears has a purpose: people live longer if they are tuned into their fears. For example, fear of fires, hurricanes, and the like can encourage preparation. That's a positive.

The problem with an overfocus on fears is that it tends to inhibit gratitude and trigger pessimism, anxiety, and depression. For our gratitude evenings, then, in the spirit of every virtue taken to its extreme becomes a vice, we focus on our gratitude for all the circumstances that allow people in developed nations who are our age today to live *twice as long* as people born 100 years before us.

We might focus on our gratitude for what we take for granted: having good-quality water available at the turn of our wrist, electricity rather than the potential asthma and health hazards of a fireplace, better sanitation, the availability of good doctors in our community, the availability of better medical devices and procedures so that an appointment with a periodontist doesn't imply surgery now as it did in the past, or the improvements in hip and knee replacements.

Gratitude finding becomes easier with a little knowledge of history combined with laughing about how many of Liz and my mini-laments are merely examples of first world problems. Instead of grousing about having to take out the garbage and separating the multiple types of recycling, worrying if I have it right and wondering whether the plastics really do get recycled, gratitude finding may include knowing that about 100 years ago, many cities did not even have garbage trucks. People dumped their garbage in backyards and parks, natural springs and streams got contaminated with animal and human wastes, and the contamination caused outbreaks of cholera and yellow fever, resulting in shorter life spans.

Just recalling this history triggers my gratitude for garbage collectors leaving their warm beds at 4 am to enter a cold, dark world, sometimes in pouring rain, sleet, or snow to spend eight hours lifting hundreds of heavy cans. And once I thought about that, I couldn't recall an article or newscast about any of them complaining. I realized my grousing was, well, twenty-first-century garbage.

Recalling history helps us put annoyances like a delayed flight into perspective: instead of taking six hours to fly from the East to the West Coast, it used to take years to get there, with a serious risk of life in the process, and arriving at an empty piece of land rather than our home.

I find gratitude finding is also facilitated by recalling my own childhood. For my dad, who was born in 1910 and had lived through two world wars and a depression by age thirty-five, even my mention of pursuing a career in writing, or any passion, was countered with, "Being a mature adult is doing what you have to do, not what you want to do."

Knowing about starving artists and that usually the more a career is fulfilling, the less it pays engenders gratitude that Liz and I can pursue a fulfilling career sustainably. And it increases my gratitude and respect for Liz to see how she has virtually run her PR firm in the medical field for 30 years, during which she was also raising children. When I home in on greater specificity for that gratitude, I recall this was even before emails, the internet, or Zoom-type communication made virtual work more viable. The gratitude, however, reappears only when we set aside the gratitude time.

As a boy of nine, I had never seen a physical TV. When my family got one, we could choose from only three networks. Today Liz and I are sometimes tempted to complain about the cost of a streaming service and the additional cost of the ad-free option more than to express gratitude for how the choice of more than two hundred services allows me to find something for any mood I wish to create or enhance without wasting a third of the hour wading through commercials.

As a teenager, if I liked a song enough to wish to hear it on command,

I would have to spend a high percentage of what I made pulling weeds or mowing lawns for one 45 record with one song per side. Today I can ask Alexa or Spotify to play whatever I want for close to nothing. And since I consider music the cheapest therapist and the healthiest drug, this is something for which I can be grateful.

When I received my master's degree from UCLA in 1966, I had never even seen a computer. Today, rather than focusing on the culture's abuses and misuses of technology, I express gratitude for the way technology has made it increasingly easy for me to work virtually from home. I recall how each of my first three books were written on thousands of 3×5 index cards wrapped in rubber bands. Each morning I would spread them out on two large tables in places from the NYU law library to the Library of Congress. For the gratitude evening, I appreciate how we take but a few seconds to google answers to questions I could previously have found only by searching through books. Similarly, I feel gratitude for how I can dictate a creative thought during a car trip into my iPhone rather than forget it by the time I get home. And as for Open AI's ChatGPT or Claude, OMG (as in "oh my gratitude")!

As an older man, I thank technology for helping us bridge the physical gap between where we live and where various members of our family live—even being able to make free calls on WhatsApp to family members even if we're in Asia. And as someone who has started hundreds of men's and women's groups, I feel gratitude for the ability of all of them to remain connected even after a member moves. As Liz and I see so many families break up, or never get formed, we are both appreciative of growing up with a devoted and loving mother and father who had high expectations and good boundary enforcement.

A gratitude evening Liz and I haven't done yet is to review the 27 categories of decisions couples typically face—the ones I suggested as candidates for the creation of win-win solutions (chapter 10). The incomplete list of more than 200 examples encourages me to focus on how grateful I am that Liz and I worked out solutions to more than 98 percent of them, rather than to focus on the 2 percent that still need solutions.

As with appreciations, the gratitude evenings require discipline. As with appreciations, they're best when they are specific. I hope all the specifics I've offered here inspire parallel specific gratitude in your life.

Of course, there is no magic to gratitude time being in the evenings: they'd also be a great way to start the day!

Chapter 6

Secret 2: The Caring and Sharing Practice

How to Handle Personal Criticism without Becoming Defensive

The Caring and Sharing Practice is the primary method of transforming our response to criticism from defensive to receptive. It is the backbone of *Role Mate to Soul Mate*.

Two warnings: First, the multiple steps in the practice (twenty-four in all) will exhaust you at the outset, but after a few times they will come more naturally. Second, the most frequent feedback I hear in my post-workshop follow-up group calls is some version of, "One week we skipped a couple of the twenty-four steps—like the one where we had to repeat the mindsets that we had just gone through a half hour before—and we just didn't feel the same degree of receptivity from each other. Now we've come to value each step. And even the repetition."

Until now, the most advanced work in communication was active listening. But both John Gottman and I found that very few couples do active listening on their own without a therapist. Why? Active listening is good for the *sharer* who feels heard when their partner says, "What I heard you say . . . ," but the person *listening* (and often feeling criticized) experiences a double jeopardy: they feel attacked without their biologically natural defenses, and therefore especially vulnerable; and their vulnerability is magnified when they are expected to repeat the criticism (by responding with, "What I heard you say . . .").

The active listener, then, experiences the double jeopardy of feeling attacked from both outside (by their partner) and inside (by themself) without their natural defenses. Anticipating this, couples avoid doing active listening unless a therapist guides them through it. And millions of couples cannot afford a therapist as frequently as they feel criticized. The ones who can afford it are often too busy making money to have the time.

The Caring and Sharing Practice is designed to facilitate a temporary work-around to this natural propensity to respond defensively to criticism, bringing about the evolutionary shift I mentioned in chapter 1. It does this via preparation preceding criticism. That is, you will be setting time aside to hear your partner's most important concern or criticism. And then **before you hear your loved one's criticism, you will prepare yourself to experience their concerns as an opportunity to feel more loved.** Feeling more loved requires no defenses.

That Superpower Feeling

Almost miraculously, a good Caring and Sharing session often leaves both partners feeling that they have acquired a superpower: knowing how to turn any future criticism into an opportunity to deepen their and their partner's love. Since experiencing personal criticism as an opportunity to deepen love is an evolutionary shift, the feeling has considerable validity. In fact, the Caring and Sharing superpower is even an evolutionary shift for superheroes, who just use their superpowers to kill the criticizer ever more efficiently!

Preparing for the Caring and Sharing Practice

Here are the five most important steps to prepare for an effective Caring and Sharing Practice:

Step 1: Schedule a Caring and Sharing Practice once per week, and set the scene.

Like Appreciations, the Caring and Sharing Practice is both an art and a discipline. As an **art**, weekly rotate the partner who will create a setting that is aesthetic, nurturing—even sacred. The ideal space is your bedroom, with some candles and flowers. As a **discipline**, it helps, but is not mandatory, to have the Caring and Sharing Practice at the same time each week. Decide on a time when you know you will have at least two hours of time undisturbed by such distractions as electronics and children. Early Sunday evening has been the most popular time for couples. Liz and I do it on Sunday morning. Be certain to schedule the next meeting proactively prior to completing each session. That is, **always have a Caring and Sharing Practice on the calendar.**

The importance of always having a Caring and Sharing Practice on the calendar is explained best by what might be called the Johns Hopkins effect. At Johns Hopkins University, a study was done of children who were fed on a predictable schedule and a control group of children fed an equal amount of food and frequency but on an unpredictable schedule. The findings? The children fed on a predictable schedule felt much more secure; the children who didn't know when they would next be fed ate frantically and tried to gobble up as much as they could.

The takeaway? When an issue comes up and you're beginning to feel the likelihood of an escalating argument, knowing that you have a Caring and Sharing Practice on your calendar during which you will feel fully heard creates the internal security that allows you not to feel frantic and in need of immediately making your point for fear that otherwise you will never be heard.

Step 2: Appreciation Preparation

The overall structure of the Caring and Sharing Practice can be thought of as a Caring and Sharing Sandwich:

Bread: Two specific appreciations
Meat (or veggies): One concern (or criticism)
Bread: Two specific appreciations

Prepare, therefore, by "baking the bread," or creating four appreciations with four to five levels of specificity as outlined in chapter 5.

Step 3: Criticism Preparation

Write down the three areas of concern (what your partner will usually label as criticism) about which you feel least understood by your partner. Each may be something you've said a hundred times because you've never felt fully heard. From among the three concerns, choose the one that once really heard would do the most to facilitate you feeling understood by your loved one, and therefore feeling a deeper love.

Sometimes I am asked, "What, just *one* concern a week? What am I going to do with the others—stuff them?"

Answer: You'll find that by feeling fully heard about your most important concern, you'll feel secure that virtually any concern you have will be heard without dealing with defensive counterattacks or a hurt loved one. You'll feel the relief of no longer having to walk on eggshells, waiting for just the right moment and mood to say what is bothering you.

Step 4: Preparing for the Six Mindsets of Receptivity with the Die for Partner Exercise

The Six Mindsets of Receptivity temporarily create an altered state of receptivity before hearing your partner's criticisms or concerns. You'll begin your altered state of receptivity not with LSD or psilocybin, but with the Die for Partner exercise.

Die for Partner

1. Grab your notepad and pen and sit *with your back to your partner* so your partner cannot see what you write.
2. Write your answer to this question: If you saw that your partner had a 100 percent chance of being killed (e.g., drowning or in a car accident) and you knew that you had a 100 percent chance of saving your partner's life but you would risk about a 50 percent chance of losing your own life, would you do it (if you had no children to consider)?

   Write "Die?" on the pad, then choose yes, no, or uncertain.
3. Draw a line under the answer to the die question and answer the same question with one change: instead of a 50 percent chance of suffering a loss of life, substitute the loss of a limb—an arm or

a leg. On the notepad, write: "Limb?" then choose yes, no, or uncertain.

The first of the Six Mindsets, then, is, "If I would risk my life to save my partner's life, the least I can do is listen!"

What do you say to your partner if you wouldn't risk your life? Say, "If I would lose an arm so you would live" or "If I would lose a leg" or choose something that you would be willing to give up to save your loved one's life (e.g., your new car, or your home) that makes listening look small by comparison.

Of interest: Although about one-third of my workshop participants are considering divorce or a breakup (versus about two-thirds who are there primarily for relationship enhancement), about 90 percent of the men and about 80 percent of the women give yes as an answer to the question of whether they would risk their life to save their partner's life (if they had no children to consider). Each of my workshop participants know their partner will never see or hear their answers. (I know the percentages because everyone tosses their answers into a corner of the room so they can be read anonymously.)

Step 5: Mastering the Six Mindsets of Receptivity

From a quarter century of feedback, the Six Mindsets have risen to the top as the ones that create the most receptivity to the experience of hearing a partner's criticism as an opportunity to feel more deeply loved.

One caveat: For most people the altered state from defensiveness to receptivity only lasts for about a half hour. You will need to repeat the Six Mindsets both before you hear your partner's criticism, and before you hear your partner's response to your concern. Note that I am calling this concern a criticism for two reasons: First, because that's the way it is likely to feel to the person hearing the concern, as we saw in chapter 3, with

"Soul-Mate Wisdom 4," of how criticism looks different to the criticizer and the criticized.

Second, because a function of the course is to prepare you to feel safe even with your partner's worst criticism and even when the criticism is given badly, and make it safe for your partner to give their worst criticism without walking on eggshells about how they give it.

Choose one of you to be the first to share their criticism. This should be the partner who is more frequently upset. This partner will be the first sharer. The other partner is the first listener.

The first listener will read the mindsets *out loud,* following these four steps:

1. Read each mindset as it is written.
2. Share your understanding of it in your own words. This increases the first sharer's feeling of safety by knowing you've *internalized* the mindset.
3. Review my version of the mindset again to see if you missed anything.
4. Share the best of my version and your version.

The Six Mindsets of Receptivity are:

1. **Die for Partner:** If I will die so you will live. The least I can do is listen to you! When you feel heard, you'll feel more alive. So another way of saying this mindset is, "If I will die so you will live. The least I can do is listen to give you life." (If you changed the statement in the Die for Partner exercise below to "I would lose a limb" or similar, you can substitute that here.)
2. **Love Guarantee:** The more I provide a safe space for all your feelings, the more you will feel loved by me and the more you will love me. (If your version is, "If I listen to you, you'll feel

loved by me," when you review your partner's version, note that you've left out "therefore, the more you will love me." If your partner knows that you understand that you will also get the benefit of feeling more loved, your partner may feel more secure. If that resonates with you, add it. If not, leave it out.)

3. **Cinematic Immersion:** First, if I feel myself getting upset, I'll tell myself it's only a movie. Since neither you nor a movie are physically hitting me, I can relax.

    Second, I'll remind myself that at a movie I don't *argue* with the actors' stories; I *immerse* myself in the actors' stories. I don't leave early; I stay to the end. I can both relax and immerse myself in your story to the end.

4. **Attach/Detach:** I cannot attach to your story until I *detach* from my defenses such as thinking to myself, "I have a response to that."

    If I can't stop listening to my defenses, I will say "Hold" until I feel fully receptive again. I will only ask you to continue when I can fully listen to you.

5. **Stream:** If I feel you are distorting or angry, I will visualize the distortion and anger as pollution in a stream. I will imagine my listening as being a *filter*, removing those impurities. I look forward to the filter of my listening restoring your Stream to its natural purity and beauty.

6. **Eye Contact:** Only after I have altered my naturally defensive mindset can my eye contact be genuinely supportive because I feel safe, therefore you are safe, and our love will deepen.

    Therapists will sometimes suggest you give your partner supportive eye contact from the outset. That can seduce your partner into opening up only to be met with a defensive counterattack. I, therefore, ask you to give supportive eye contact only after the first five mindsets have allowed you to fully alter your mindset from defensive to receptive.

A mnemonic for the Six Mindsets is a CASE of dying for love:

C = Cinematic Immersion
A = Attach/Detach
S = Stream
E = Eye contact
Dying for love = Die for Partner and the Love Guarantee

I am often asked, "While my partner is reading the mindsets, can I say anything?" No. You are just watching your partner feel safe. **If your partner doesn't feel safe, you aren't safe.** The Six Mindsets keep both of you safe.

"Hold"

One word, "Hold," is also pivotal in keeping both of you safe. When you find yourself contemplating a response—or self-listening—say "Hold." Especially if you are making a mental note to respond to that point when your partner is finished.

After you say Hold, recenter yourself. Most participants do this by recalling a mindset or two that works best to recenter them. Some mindsets will be helpful right away (e.g., Love Guarantee and Die for Partner), and others will be helpful after you work on them for a while (e.g., Stream). Keep experimenting.

Saying Hold is a way of honoring your partner. It signals your desire to be 100 percent focused and to exert the self-discipline to recenter yourself when you lose 100 percent focus. After you say Hold, tell your partner when you are centered again and ready for your partner to continue. If you suddenly recall that you have to pack for a trip or do something necessary that will prevent you from focusing on the Caring and Sharing Practice, be sure to reschedule the session prior to ending it.

Notes? Do not take notes, even with the positive intent of not wanting to miss anything. They aren't needed because after the exercise, the listener will ask the sharer, "Did I miss anything?" I made this part of the process because I found that taking notes is distracting to both partners.

The Detective-Therapist Mindset

The Detective-Therapist mindset is extremely helpful to some people, but less so to others. Feel free to add it or consider substituting it for Stream or Cinematic Immersion if it works better for you than either of those. The Detective mindset goes something like this:

I am a detective searching for every piece of your puzzle until I see your full picture. To discover every piece, I must be curious. I will keep drawing you out until you are thinking thoughts you didn't even know you were thinking. My goal? To see your whole picture as clearly as you see it. My litmus test? When I've got the puzzle right, I'll see why your picture looks the way it does. Then I can genuinely say, "Now I see how that makes sense [to you]."

For a detective, the usual goal is to prosecute. Since the goal here is to piece together the virtue behind what appears to be your nemesis' vice, your goal is more like that of a therapist.

After Sharing: How the Listener Makes the Sharer Feel Heard

During the Sharing and Caring Practice, when your partner says they are finished sharing their criticism, you'll say:

1. **What I heard you *say* was** . . . (share the best intent of what you heard).
2. **Did I *distort* anything?**
3. **Did I *miss* anything?** (Do not ask this until your partner says nothing was distorted.)
4. **Is there anything new you'd like to *add*?** Avoid the "add" for the first few months. After that, it is optional—only if there is time and energy. You can always bring the same topic up another week.

Mnemonic: Say like a cheerleader: I say, you say, DMA (If it helps you remember "DMA," you might think direct memory access, or designated market areas).

When It's Time for the Listener's Response

When your partner says they feel completely heard, then it's your turn to respond—but not with your separate concern; you'll bring that up after your partner hears your response to their concern. To prepare to hear your response, your partner will read the Six Mindsets aloud in the same way you did.

Since all this can be overwhelming, I'll walk you through it step-by-step. See the next page.

The Caring and Sharing Practice Step-by-Step

The step-by-step part of this chapter is most easily used if both partners have a copy of the steps. This portion of the chapter is available to print out from the beginning of the online video version of the "Role Mate to Soul Mate" course. (See the final page of the book for the QR code.)

Decide which partner is more frequently upset. This partner will be sharing the first concern. The first sharer will be called Partner One.

Partner One will play three roles in this order—sharer, responder, listener—and will always be called Partner One.

Partner Two will also play three roles but in this order—listener, responder, sharer—and will always be called Partner Two.

Partner One should first choose the concern that if fully understood will make them feel the most loved by Partner Two.

Step 1

Partner One (First Sharer): Start with the "bread" of the Caring and Sharing Sandwich: that is, share two **appreciations**; try to get to **specificity level 3 or more.**

Partner Two (First Listener): Soak it up.

Step 2

Partner One: Listen to your partner review the Six Mindsets *out loud* so you feel safe because your partner feels safe.

Partner Two: Read the Six Mindsets out loud to your partner. For each mindset:

1. Read the mindset as written.
2. Say the mindset in your own words.
3. Ask yourself, "Am I missing anything?"
4. Add what you missed.

Make sure you're feeling both centered and safe before you tell Partner One, "OK, I'm ready." Remember to say "Hold" whenever you catch yourself self-listening.

Step 3

Partner One: Share your concern/criticism. Be specific. Share how it makes you feel. Elaborate but stay with feelings that emanate *directly* from that concern/criticism. For example, "When you buy a new car without asking me, it makes me feel like I'm not a partner," can be followed by, "and it brings back the trauma of my first marriage." But "When you buy a new car . . ." should *not* be followed by "I *also* don't like it when you seem to be stricter with my child from my first marriage than yours from your first marriage." Save that for the next Caring and Sharing session.

Partner Two: 100 percent listening. If you catch yourself thinking of a response to your partner's perspective (self-listening) remember, "This is the story of the one I love; to listen is to give my loved one life."

If that doesn't recenter you, say "Hold." Recenter yourself with your most centering mindset(s).

Do not take notes to recall what your partner says. At step 5, you'll be asking, "Did I miss anything?" Your partner will be happy to repeat what you missed. Your partner is given life by your focus and supportive eye contact, nothing else.

Step 4

Partner One: Thank your partner for listening.

Partner Two: Say, "What I *heard you say* was . . . ," and share whatever you can recall.

Step 5

Partner Two: When finished sharing whatever you recall from Partner One's account, ask, "Is there anything you feel I *distorted*?"

If Partner One's answer is no, skip to step 6. If their answer is yes, read on.

Partner One: Share what you feel was distorted, and what you were trying to say.

Partner Two: Whether or not you feel you did in fact distort, keep working at it until your partner says they feel you got it with no distortion.

Step 6

Partner Two: Ask, "Did I *miss* anything?"

If Partner One's answer is no, skip to step 7. If their answer is yes, read on.

Partner One: Share what you feel was missed.

Partner Two: Do not say, "Now I understand." "I understand" and "got it" are often euphemisms for "shut up." Keep sharing with Partner One exactly what you feel you understand until your partner says they feel understood. That is, your partner is the one who gives the "Now-I-really-feel-understood" award!

Once Partner One feels nothing was either distorted or missed, then it is Partner Two's turn to respond. But first, **an important side note:**

Partner One, please take a moment to *read* the following paragraphs *out loud* to your loved one:

"It is natural to feel that a byproduct of you understanding me is that you will basically agree with me. If, however, you paint a very different picture, I will recall Soul-Mate Wisdom 2 that the choice of my partner is my most important single statement as to the choice of my values. I will remind myself by looking at this image:"

These four illustrations are the way illustrator Thomas Fuchs imagined that Mario Cuomo, the former governor of New York, would be depicted by, clockwise from top left, Andy Warhol, Pablo Picasso, Piet Mondrian, and Robert Crumb.

Continue by saying, "I am noting that all four pictures are of the same man (Mario Cuomo) at the exact same moment yet are nevertheless viewed very differently.

"I will respect that the very qualities for which I chose you also create a filter through which you see a different picture even when we are looking at the same one. Even if in places your view contradicts mine, I will be at peace with our contradictions coexisting. It is the picture seen by the person who is willing to risk their life for me."

———

Finally, a touch of irony: note that among the pictures of Mario Cuomo, the picture that appears most distorted is likely the one that is most *valued*—it is the illustrator's depiction of how *Picasso* might have portrayed Mario Cuomo! Don't undervalue your partner's distortions!

OK, now you're ready to hear your partner's response. Note that the responder, Partner Two, does not have to give two appreciations first (for the Caring and Sharing Sandwich). That only needs to be done prior to sharing your main concern or criticism.

Step 7

Partner Two (was first listener, now responder): Listen to your loved one review the Six Mindsets out loud so you feel safe because your partner feels safe.

Partner One (was first sharer, now listener): Read out loud to your partner the Six Mindsets. For each mindset:

1. Read the mindset as written.
2. Say the mindset in your own words.
3. Ask yourself, "Am I missing anything?"
4. Add what you missed.

Make sure you're feeling both centered and safe before you tell Partner Two, "OK, I'm ready." Remember to say Hold whenever you catch yourself "self-listening" or being distracted.

Step 8

Partner Two: Share your version of Partner One's concern or criticism. (Remember, this is *not* your own primary concern. You'll share that after you have responded to your partner's concern.)

Partner One: 100 percent listening. If you catch yourself thinking of a flaw in your partner's perspective, remember, "This is the **story**

of the one I love; to listen is to give my partner life." If that doesn't recenter you, say Hold. Recenter yourself with your most centering mindset(s).

Do not take notes to recall what your partner says. At step 11 you'll be asking, "Did I miss anything?" Your partner will be happy to repeat what you missed. Your partner is given life by your focus and supportive eye contact, nothing else.

Step 9

Partner Two: Thank your partner for listening.

Partner One: Say, "What I *heard you say* was . . . ," and share whatever you can recall.

Step 10

Partner One: When finished recounting your version of Partner Two's account, ask, "Is there anything you feel I *distorted*?"

If their answer is no, skip to step 11. If their answer is yes, read on.

Partner Two: Share what you feel was distorted and what you were trying to say.

Partner One: Do not say, "Now I understand." "I understand" and "got it" are often euphemisms for "shut up." Keep sharing with Partner Two exactly what you feel you understand until your partner says they feel understood. That is, your partner is the one who gives the "Now-I-really-feel-understood" award!

Step 11

Partner One: Ask, "Did I miss anything?"

If their answer is no, skip to step 12. If their answer is yes, read on.

Partner Two: Share what you feel was missed.

Partner One: Keep sharing with Partner Two exactly what they feel was missed until they give you the Understand award!

You've just put into practice an evolutionary shift by handling personal criticism from your loved one without being defensive (and hopefully without feeling defensive).

So stand up and give each other a big hug!

Step 12

Partner Two (originally the First Listener and is now the Second Sharer): Share two appreciations; try to get to specificity level 3 or more.

Partner One (originally the First Sharer and is now the Second Listener): Soak it up.

Step 13

Partner Two: Listen to Partner One review the Six Mindsets out loud so you feel safe because your partner feels safe.

Partner One: Read out loud to Partner Two the Six Mindsets. For each mindset:

1. Read the mindset as written.
2. Say the mindset in your own words.
3. Ask yourself, "Am I missing anything?"
4. Add what you missed.

Make sure you're feeling both centered and safe before you tell your partner, "OK, I'm ready." Remember to say "Hold" whenever you catch yourself self-listening.

Step 14

Partner Two: Share your concern/criticism. Be specific. Share how it makes you feel. Elaborate but stay with feelings that emanate *directly* from that concern/criticism. For example, "When you buy a new car without asking me, it makes me feel like I'm not a partner," can be followed by, "and it brings back the trauma of my first marriage." But "When you buy a new car" should *not* be followed by "I also don't like it when you seem to be stricter with my child from my first marriage than yours from your first marriage." Save that for the next Caring and Sharing session.

Partner One: 100 percent listen. If you catch yourself thinking of a flaw in your partner's perspective, remember, "This is the story of the one I love; to listen is to give my partner life."

If that doesn't recenter you, say Hold. Recenter yourself with your most centering mindset(s).

Step 15

Partner Two: Thank your partner for listening.
Partner One: Say, "What I *heard you say* was . . ."

Step 16

Partner One: When finished sharing your version of Partner Two's account, ask, "Is there anything you feel I *distorted*?"
If their answer is no, skip to step 17. If their answer is yes, read on.
Partner Two: Share what you feel was distorted and what you were trying to say.
Partner One: Whether or not you feel you did in fact distort, keep working at it until your partner says they feel understood.

Step 17

Partner One: Ask, "Did I *miss* anything?"

If Partner Two's answer is no, skip to step 18. If their answer is yes, read on.

Partner Two: Share what you feel was missed.

Partner One: Keep sharing with Partner Two exactly what they feel was missed until they say they feel understood.

Great, you're almost there! (Now you know why I call this a "Discipline"!) OK, Couple's Last Stand . . .

Step 18

Partner One (Originally the "First Sharer," is now "Second Responder"): Listen to your partner review mindsets out loud so that you feel safe because your partner feels safe.

Partner Two (Originally the "First Listener," is now the "Final Listener"): You'll be tempted by now to give the Six Mindsets short shrift—or even just say, "I've just gone over them—I've got it; go ahead." Recall that the mindsets only last about a half hour—you are counterprogramming your brain with the evolutionary shift from defensiveness to receptivity. Give your partner the security of you reviewing them anew; your partner will feel safer as they see you renew your safety.

Read out loud to your partner the Six Mindsets. For each mindset:

1. Read the mindset as written.
2. Say it in your own words.
3. Ask yourself, "Am I missing anything?"
4. Add what you missed.

Make sure you're feeling both centered and safe before you tell your partner, "OK, I'm ready."

Step 19

Partner One: Share your version of your partner's concern or criticism.

Partner Two: 100 percent listen. Remember the visual of the four different views of Mario Cuomo, and your choice of your partner being a reflection of what you value.

Step 20

Partner One: Thank your partner for listening.

Partner Two: Say, "What *I heard you say* was . . ."

Step 21

Partner Two: When finished sharing your version of Partner One's account, ask, "Is there anything you feel I *distorted*?"

If their answer is no, skip to step 22. If their answer is yes, read on.

Partner One: Share what you feel was **distorted,** and what you were trying to say.

Partner Two: Even if you feel you did not distort, keep working at it until *your partner* says she or he feels understood.

Step 22

Partner Two: Ask, "Did I **miss** anything?"

If their answer is no, skip to step 23. If their answer is yes, read on.

Partner One: Share what you feel was missed.

Partner Two: Keep sharing with Partner One exactly what they feel was missed until they say they feel understood.

Step 23

Partner One: Share with Partner Two:

1. What Partner Two shared about their concern that you appreciate now more than ever.
2. What Partner Two said to make you feel heard about your concern.

Partner Two: Share with Partner One:

1. What your partner shared about their concern that you appreciate now more than ever.
2. What your partner said to make you feel heard about your concern.

Step 24

Each share **two specific appreciations** with your partner to complete the Caring and Sharing Sandwich.

———

You've just completed the discipline of hearing and responding to each other's concerns without either of you becoming defensive. Stand up and give your partner a big hug. No, no. A *bigger* hug!

Chapter 7

Secret 3: Creating and Sustaining a Conflict-Free Zone, Including the Four-Part Apology

You've set aside 2 hours per week to do your Caring and Sharing Practice. That leaves 166 hours per week for potential conflict. Assuming your partnership vows don't include "In hopes of frequent conflict and mutual alienation," let's set up your Conflict-Free Zone.

The Conflict-Free Zone is about preventing criticisms from escalating into a conflict. Note that I did not say that the Conflict-Free Zone is a *criticism*-free zone. (We saw how in chapter 2, "The Four Depleters of Love," even though the criticizer does not see themselves as a criticizer but rather as merely suggesting changes that will *increase* intimacy, that nevertheless the person hearing their loved one make any suggestion for a change in attitude or behavior often experiences it as criticism.)

If that applies to you, you will experience criticism during the week (assuming you communicate with your partner!). Here are the ways to nevertheless both create and sustain the Conflict-Free Zone.

The Seven Core Methods to Prevent Criticism from Escalating into Conflict

Method One: Visualize Two Options

When your partner criticizes you, **visualize two options:**

Option One: Visualize, "I can wait until the Caring and Sharing session, when we'll both be *heard."*

Option Two: Visualize, "I can respond immediately, and we'll both be *hurt."*

Jim and Jan give us a clear example.

"You left the toilet seat up again," Jan reminded Jim.

Jim rolled his eyes and bristled to himself, *I just finished shopping, rushed back here to use the bathroom, and hurried back out to put the ice cream in the freezer. And the only thing you can say is "You left the toilet seat up"?*

But out loud, Jim said nothing. He was proud of his restraint.

A few seconds later, Jan dutifully hurried to help him put the rest of the groceries away. In the process she noted, "Oh, you got the wrong-sized carton of milk—the gallon size makes the fridge too crowded."

Agitated about the toilet seat criticism from a minute before, Jim didn't hesitate to shoot back in a tone reflecting his agitation. "The gallon size saves us money, and you're always complaining that when I shop, I'm not conscious of prices." Now he was on roll. "And besides, with all your self-righteousness about the environment, you'd think you'd know that two containers are more landfill than one. I'm damned if I do, and damned if I don't."

Jan shot back, "Self-righteous? I merely ask you to get a different size container of milk and suddenly I'm self-righteous? I can't even make a little suggestion around you—talk about a fragile ego."

What would have averted this from battle zone to Conflict-Free Zone? Either Jan or Jim visualizing, *I can wait until the Caring and Sharing session, and we'll both be heard.*

In the Caring and Sharing session, Jan would have first prepared herself to hear not only Jim's agitation about the toilet seat criticism, but also to provide a safe environment for him to share how the real issue was what Jim felt was Jan's propensity to pan for criticisms, rather than pan for gold.

Note that it only would have taken one partner to visualize the value of option one. Which implies that **once both partners make the commitment to visualize taking a response to criticism to Caring and Sharing rather than respond defensively, any fight is the responsibility of both partners.**

However, if you choose the win-win option, what do you do between the criticism and the Caring and Sharing time? Too many couples stomach it, which is like depositing poison into every cell of your body. It ultimately damages both physical and mental health. It may manifest as passive-aggressiveness or it may, as with Jim and Jan, erupt into a volcano of rage catalyzed by a small event that triggers the release of all the pent-up resentment.

Instead of confronting, or stomaching it, there's a better alternative: Journaling.

Method Two: Journaling

Journaling is like the first half hour with a therapist, but it's free. Abe Lincoln had myriad critics. He "responded" by writing vehement letters, then putting them aside. The process gave him solace.

Journaling is best done in four stages:

1. **Self-Righteous Stage:** Write out why you are 100 percent right, as well as everything your partner doesn't get. This is the biologically natural stage. Let it give you solace without guilt.

2. **The Crack in the Self-Righteous Stage:** Write down just one thing you could have said or done differently.

3. **Introspection Stage:** Write down everything you could have said or done differently.

4. **Empathy Stage:** Write down your partner's perspective. Think about what your partner would say were your partner writing their perspective, and what you can ultimately empathize with when you view their way.

When you review what you wrote, the first self-righteous stage will bring you an internal smile of humility and begin to reprogram your brain so in the future you will be able to visualize the succeeding stages when you feel you are 100 percent right.

Method Three: Pray or Meditate

Praying, meditating, and journaling all offer the solace of expressing our feelings and doing so confidentially. With both meditating and praying you are calling on wisdom—either wisdom from within or wisdom from above.

Method Four: Use Notes to Self

Place Post-its or index cards throughout the house in places you feel you are most likely to experience negative feelings but where they will not be seen by your loved one. That might be on a night table near your bed or in the bathroom so you don't forget the ruminations you may have experienced in the shower. Create appreciations from the positive; save the negative for the Caring and Sharing session.

Method Five: Fake it 'til you make it

For example, when upset, buy your partner flowers, offer a shoulder rub, cook dinner, make a favorite dessert, or leave a note of appreciation. As you fake it, you'll anticipate your partner's appreciation, and that will soften your agitation.

Method Six: The Aikido Reflex

During a Caring and Sharing session, Ashley shared with Chris, "When you criticize me, it feels like you've shot an arrow into my heart, and I can't get it out. I try to get rid of it by criticizing you back, but then you just shoot me with another arrow."

I asked everyone in the workshop to stand up and think of a criticism their partner sometimes gives them that stings. Then I asked them to imagine, as in the martial art aikido, that when their partner shoots criticism at them, they allow *the energy of that criticism* to pass right through them and out the other side, disappearing into the night.

Like aikido, it takes some practice because a fundamental teaching of aikido is to overcome oneself, or, in this context, to overcome the natural tendency to let the arrow stick in you, and instead master allowing the negative energy to go through you to be lost in the ether.

As each couple practiced that in the workshop by "shooting" their partner with a mild criticism, most couples were able to get it at least partially. A few said it almost completely prevented the pain and therefore their desire to defend and destroy "the enemy" with their own arrow.

The Aikido Reflex doesn't have to stand alone. Even if it only reduces the sting, it can relax you enough for you to visualize your response being heard in Caring and Sharing and in the meantime employing the four stages of journaling.

Method Seven: Turn On the Music

Music is your cheapest therapist and your healthiest drug. Few things can affect your energy more quickly than music—especially your favorite romantic songs and high-energy music. In my workshops, I begin each session with high-energy music to which everyone dances, and end the workshops with a romantic, soul mate–enhancing song. Jump-start the process with this music exercise.

The Music Exercise

Write down your two favorite romantic songs and your two favorite high-energy (anti-depressant) songs. Exchange them with your partner. Put your partner's favorites on your preferred app's (Spotify, Pandora, Apple) playlist. Play one of your partner's favorite songs when they are feeling low in energy or upset about the relationship.

———

These seven methods are what couples report to be the best ways to both sustain and fortify their Conflict-Free Zone.

However, it is not a criticism but a caring question that often slips through the cracks of the Conflict-Free Zone. It is the "Are-You-OK?" question. The solution? The "Are-You-OK?" Agreement.

The "Are-You-OK?" Agreement

Jessica had just returned from taking the kids to school. As she hung up her jacket, she sensed Michael breathing slightly differently than his norm. She asked, "Are you OK?"

Michael answered, "Yeah, just a little rushed for work."

Jessica knew that Michael was rushed for work most every morning yet still felt his breathing pattern was different than it was even under those circumstances.

"No, it's more than that. What's going on?"

Michael finally let it out, "I was just feeling that you're always over-protecting the kids. It's healthier for them to walk a few blocks to school than to be taken there by mom the limo driver."

"It's more than a few blocks. It's practically a half mile. And it's cold. Why are you begrudging them a ride? Why don't you get up earlier like I do so *you* can take them?"

Jessica and Michael's dialogue escalated into an argument that soured their day. Their Conflict-Free Zone became a battle zone.

Both Jessica and Michael could have avoided this, each in their own way, by creating an "Are-You-OK?" agreement. The agreement creates a discipline for both partners.

For the Asker

If you've lived with your partner for a while, the combination of your partner's tone of voice, body language, and even breathing patterns allows you to sense with about 80 percent accuracy when something is not OK. Before you ask, "Are you OK?" or "Is anything the matter?" or "Is something wrong?", just assume that something *is* wrong, and if you're right, there's about a 70 percent chance that *you* are part of the problem. Therefore, take a few seconds prior to asking your partner if they're OK to prepare yourself in two ways:

1. Reflect on one or two mindsets (e.g., Die for Partner or the Love Guarantee) that you feel are most likely to center you enough so

you won't feel defensive even if you hear that you are the reason your partner is not OK.

2. Visualize this backup plan should that mindset not work: Imagine suggesting calmly, "Let's Hold. I know I'll be able to listen to you better in Caring and Sharing."

For the Asked

If you are the one being asked, then if what's bothering you has anything to do with your partner, respond with, "Let me do some journaling first and see if it's a candidate for Caring and Sharing. I know you'll hear me best then."

Note that both of you has an opportunity to prevent the Conflict-Free Zone from becoming a battle zone. Therefore, if the Conflict-Free Zone does become a battle zone, whose fault is it?

————

In reality, the Conflict-Free Zone can still occasionally become a battle zone. One of the most effective ways of averting the battle zone, while deepening both your love and respect for each other, is mastering the Four-Part Apology.

The Four-Part Apology

"Love means never having to say you're sorry." Or so we heard from Ryan O'Neal's character in *Love Story*. Aside from that being a perfect example of the Higher Expectations Trap, let's check out whether that is even a love-enhancing goal.

When someone apologizes to you, do you:

- feel more respected by that person? Yes/No
- increase your respect *for* that person? Yes/No
- feel acknowledged? Yes/No
- relinquish your desire to attack or defend? Yes/No
- feel less stressed? Yes/No

When your *loved one* apologizes to you, do you feel empowered in all five of those ways? Do you also:

- feel more loved *by* your partner? Yes/No
- feel more love *for* your partner? Yes/No

Almost everyone answers yes to all seven questions. Yet we often find it hard to apologize. Even to our loved one. No, *especially* to our loved one.

Even among the few of us who do manage to sputter out an apology in response to a criticism, we're down to about 0 percent of us who offer what I call a Four-Part Apology.

Introducing the Four-Part Apology

Most criticisms beg for an apology. But for some criticisms, like "You got the wrong-sized carton of milk," "You got the wrong kind of coffee at the store," for example, an "Oh, sorry" will suffice. Some criticisms, though, are more complex and also beg for a more immediate response, such as Emily's criticism of Jacob.

As Emily, Jacob, and their daughter, Krista, were enjoying dinner, Emily mentioned to Jacob, "You put the lightweight coat on Krista this morning, and she told me she was cold."

If Jacob just waits for Caring and Sharing time to give his side of the story, it can leave Krista feeling he doesn't much care. A quick "Oh, sorry," doesn't reflect much concern. So Jacob called upon the Four-Part Apology.

Jacob's tone of voice reflected concern as he said, "I'm sorry. Yeah, I don't want Krista to catch a cold. I'll check the temperature more carefully in the future."

Can you identify the **four parts** to Jacob's apology?

1. Jacob's "I'm sorry" was not followed by an excuse
2. Jacob volunteered the reason he felt the criticism was valid (his daughter could catch cold)
3. Jacob offered what he planned to do differently next time (check the temperature)
4. His tone of voice reflected a genuine concern rather than dismissiveness

Since responding with the Four-Part Apology is ideally done with some spontaneity, you need to work on the discipline of immediately accessing a mindset that will help you make a quick transition from defensiveness to the Four-Part Apology. For most couples, either the Die for Partner mindset or the Love Guarantee works best.

And since it will be easy to forget the four parts, especially following a criticism, I suggest a mnemonic. Mnemonics are best remembered when they're outrageous. Since when we're criticized we have to deal with defensiveness, EVFT (Every Effing Time or if you want to keep it clean, Every Future Time) might work.

EVFT:

E is for "**excuse**," as in no excuse

V is for acknowledging the criticism's **validity**

F is for the **future**, when you'll do what you were criticized for differently

T is for your **tone** of voice

The Four-Part Apology will not come naturally. It is a classic example of how sustaining love and deepening respect is biologically unnatural and therefore requires discipline. Giving the Four-Part Apology gift immediately after a criticism will require even more discipline than the Caring and Sharing Practice because you'll have so little time to prepare yourself.

Is it worth it? The Four-Part Apology makes your partner feel heard and acknowledged, and it increases both your partner's respect and love for you. It is perhaps the most effective one-step method of making the transition from role mate to soul mate.

Chapter 8

Secret 4: The Magic of the Ask

Remember how Jan reminding Jim that he left the toilet seat up again was the beginning of the end of their Conflict-Free Zone? Let's take a look at what that would feel like as an Ask.

The Ask

"You left the toilet seat up again," is a **criticism**.

"I love the aesthetics of the toilet seat being down. Would you be good enough to leave the toilet seat down?" is an **Ask**.

Had Jan said, "Remember, I told you before that I love the aesthetics of the toilet seat being down," that would have been a **criticism** (*"Remember, I told you before…"*) that would have ruined the Ask even if it had been followed by an Ask.

Let's deconstruct how and why the Ask could have preserved Jim and Jan's Conflict-Free Zone:

1. **Problem vs. Solution:** "I love the aesthetics of the toilet seat being down" puts the emphasis on the solution (toilet seat down), not on the problem (toilet seat up).

2. **Personal Preference vs. One Right Way:** "You left the toilet seat up again" implies that there is a right and a wrong way of leaving the toilet seat—and Jim did it the wrong way. Even if the EOT (the Encyclopedia of Toilets, of course!) said that leaving the toilet seat up was, in fact, the wrong way, when encyclopedic-type citations are used to prove how wrong we are, it just feels like a knife digging deeper into our fresh wound.

   "I love the aesthetics of the toilet seat being down" is not debatable. Who is going to argue with their loved one about their aesthetic preference? If we are willing to risk our lives to save our loved one, it's unlikely we will argue with them about their aesthetic preference.

3. **Tossing in a Criticism with the Ask:** "Remember, I told you before that . . ." is a criticism embedded in the Ask that will not inspire our partner to care about our Ask.

4. **Timing:** If Jan gave herself an hour before she mentioned her toilet seat annoyance or first journaled her annoyance, the issue would likely have evaporated.

   But if it didn't, saving it for Caring and Sharing time would allow Jan to share what was really bothering her.

When I asked Jan what that might have looked like had she saved it for Caring and Sharing, she responded, "I think the real issue is my feeling that Jim sometimes repeatedly ignores me. It makes me feel like, well, chopped liver. And certainly not like someone for whom he would risk his life."

In brief, **instead of the criticism that upsets you, do an Ask for a criticism-free solution that will make you happy.**

The Ask Exercise: You got the wrong-sized carton of milk

1. Write on a notepad the way you might apply the Ask method to Jan's comment, "You got the wrong-sized carton of milk."
2. Discuss your Ask with your partner. See if you can together create an Ask that would feel optimal to both of you. If not, rehearse in your mind's eye the style that would be optimal for your partner.

Here is a possibility for an Ask: "Can we get the quart size of milk? *I find it easier* to fit in the fridge."

What is the difference between "I find it easier" and "it is easier"? "It is easier" positions itself as a statement of fact. "I find it easier" is a statement of personal preference. When we're willing to risk our life to save our partner's life, we're usually willing to do something that makes life easier for our partner—especially when they ask.

Two other considerations would have helped make the "You got the wrong-sized carton of milk" feel more like an Ask than a criticism. First, by panning for gold; second, by timing the Ask.

Panning for Gold (Revisited)

We first discussed the idea of panning for gold in chapter 5, with the first secret, Appreciations and Gratitude. This practice can also play a part in a successful Ask. How? Let's say Jim picked up 32 items while shopping. That means 31 were potentially exactly what Jan wanted. **Before focusing on which one was "wrong," pan for gold—find one of the other 31 items that Jim did especially well:** for examples, tracking down a hard-to-find item; or getting two of an on-sale item? If none of the 31 items stands out, switch gears: did Jim forfeit something he might have preferred doing in order to shop? **Appreciating what is done right can lessen the sting of being asked to do something differently.**

If you pan for gold, you may or may not find gold. But if you don't pan for gold, you're guaranteed not to find any.

Timing the Ask for the Moment of Need

Had Jan just saved her quart of milk Ask for the time of the next shopping trip and then put "quart of milk" on the shopping list, it would never have had to be presented as something that Jim did wrong. A little patience and timing the Ask for the moment of need would have given Jan her outcome and also have served to extend the Conflict-Free Zone. And if you start a new shopping list shortly after the last shopping trip was completed, you won't have to worry about forgetting your Ask.

Combining Patience with Panning for Gold

In a private session with Frank and Phil, Phil complained, "Frank is always leaving dishes in the sink. It makes the whole kitchen look like such a mess."

Frank countered, "It's more efficient to leave some dishes in the sink because you can see how best to load the dishwasher rather than loading them right away and then readjusting them one or more times."

I asked Phil, "Does Frank always leave the dishes in the sink?"

"Not always, but most of the time."

I then asked Phil to use a combination of patience—timing the Ask— and panning for gold.

"Phil, wait for a time when Frank does put the dishes in the dishwasher and then pan for gold by either noticing which dishes he put in as he is doing it, or waiting 'til he leaves and checking the dishwasher to see which dishes he put in. Then consciously watch for that time when your appreciation can best be heard, like maybe at dinner, and share something like, 'I was stressed at work today, and it so reduced my stress when I came into the kitchen and saw that you had put the breakfast dishes in the dishwasher, and the sink was so clean. I felt peace and the love behind your thoughtfulness. Thank you.'"

Phil repeated the plan to make sure he got it right. I then added, "One caveat, Phil. Do not say, 'I love that you put the dishes in the dishwasher *rather than* leaving them in the sink.'"

Phil questioned, "Why? Doesn't that reinforce the distinction between the good and the bad?"

I explained. "It undermines an appreciation to remind your partner of what you have criticized. Leave Frank with a pure 24 karats of gold, not 12 karats diluted with 12 alloys."

Phil thought for a second, then affirmed with a smile, "Got it."

Whether it's employing some patience to time our Asks for the moment of need rather than the moment of the mistake, or panning for gold prior to "panning for fault" or expressing our Ask as a personal preference rather than as the right way to do it, each of these, and especially all of them combined, serve not only to extend our Conflict-Free Zone, but also to avoid the depletion of our reservoir of love.

Chapter 9

Secret 5: Couples Who Play Together Stay Together

Bonding via Play, Whimsies, Dancing, Roughhousing, and Teasing

When you pan for your partner's gold via Appreciations plus the gold in life via Gratitude, you're finding what is already there. When you practice being specific, you're polishing what you find.

Those are two ways of filling the reservoir of love. And there's a third way: *creating* the gold, or creating soul-mate gold. Playing together is likely the best supplement in that transition to soul mate. Couples who play together tend to stay together.

Being playful and whimsical fills the reservoir of love with excitement and a type of magic. So does dancing. Roughhousing and teasing with the kids, as well as playful sarcasm, can either fill the reservoir of love or deplete it. In this chapter we'll explore how to use roughhousing, teasing, and playful sarcasm with kids to fill the reservoir of love.

Creating Soul-Mate Gold: Being Playful and Whimsical

Dave and Sharon offer some good examples.

At a reunion of my Midland Park (New Jersey) high school graduating class of 1961, I shared with Dave Kay, one of my best high school friends, and his wife, Sharon, that I was writing this book. The response I am used to is some version of, "Boy, we could really use that, eh, honey?" followed by an admission, "Especially that part about becoming defensive when criticized—I'm afraid that's me."

Dave's response was different. "I have never ever been happier than I am now—and I've felt this way since the day I met Sharon. We've now been married for 17 years!" Sharon concurred.

Picking up on the *Role Mate to Soul Mate* title of the book, Dave added, "We were best friends from the start; she was that huge part of my heart I didn't know I was missing."

Since *falling in love* is biologically natural, I'd often encountered couples who said that when they first fell in love, they felt like soul mates. However, since *sustaining love* is biologically *un*natural, it is unusual for a couple to declare 17 years later that they still feel like soul mates. Usually, the Four Depleters of Love discussed in chapter 2 drain a couple's reservoir of love and that initial soul-mate feeling. With my curiosity piqued, I asked them for an interview.

Dave and Sharon agreed that their key to discovering their soul mate started with honesty—that is, being "brutally honest with ourselves as we filled out eHarmony's extensive questionnaire about who we are and what we want in a partner." They both disciplined themselves to refrain from giving disingenuous answers to try to make themselves look better. Their reward was that the eHarmony algorithm ranked both as their number one match for each other.

But their real contribution was how they *sustained* love. Their thick book of mementos started with the receipt from their first date. It was filled with playful and often clever appreciations of each other that were part of their everyday life. Some were sweet; others were punny and playful. For example, Sharon gave Dave a card saying, "What a difference a Dave makes."

In addition to overtly appreciating each other, they engage in frequent and creative playfulness—what they call whimsy. Here are some examples:

- On one of their first vacation trips together, Dave and Sharon stopped at a fast-food restaurant. After bringing the tray of food to their table, Dave went back for some creamer for their coffee. Upon returning, he handed the top sleeve of hash browns to Sharon, leaving the bottom sleeve for himself. Then he discovered a big bite had been taken out of his hash browns. Upset by this "unacceptable nonsense in the kitchen," he picked up the tray to show the manager. Sharon—laughing—had to hold him back while telling him the bite was hers!

- Sharon and Dave love their morning coffee. Their deal: whoever gets up first, makes it first. Early one morning, however, Dave heard Sharon go into the bathroom. He shot out of bed, started the coffeemaker, and rushed back to bed before Sharon came out, pretending he'd been sleeping the whole time. The cry of surprise when Sharon went to start the coffee that "no one" had already started turned out to be more memorable than the coffee!

- As Dave was mowing the lawn, he discovered two stunning mushrooms that seemed to have shot up overnight. Excited, he invited Sharon to share his delight and bring their camera. Sharon did indeed share in his delight as she watched him realize those mushrooms were so perfect because they were *ceramic* mushrooms she had "planted" for Dave to discover.

As for that thick book of memorabilia, it includes newspaper clippings announcing that Dave and Sharon had been chosen as eHarmony's 2006 Success Story of the Year for Pennsylvania. No surprise there.

———

We've seen how in most relationships the reservoir of love is depleted by complacency—recall the Barbra Streisand and Neil Diamond song "You Don't Bring Me Flowers." **Whimsy is complacency's antidote.** It catalyzes the healing power of laughter. It embeds memories. It makes your partner feel thought of. It keeps your relationship fresh. You never know when, where, or how you will be surprised.

Well, hopefully you are inspired. For the next edition of *Soul Mate*, email me a whimsy you create at warren@warrenfarrell.com. (I read and respond to all my emails.)

Creating Soul-Mate Gold: Dancing

While calming classical music can enhance intimacy during dinner, few things create a more effective catalyst for playfulness than high-energy dancing music. Whether it's some of the high-energy songs from Taylor Swift or Paul Simon's Graceland album or any of the high-energy music I employ in my live workshops (from Creedence Clearwater's "Proud Mary" to the Bee Gees' "Stayin' Alive," to Jerry Lee Lewis's "Great Balls of Fire"), the playfulness of dance promotes togetherness.

One of the nice things about dancing at home is that you can use the comfort of home to experiment with a crazier type of dance that you might be embarrassed to risk in public. The result? Instead of the comfort at home morphing into complacency, the comfort at home allows for an emergence out of complacency. In this ironic way, dancing is also complacency's antidote.

When Liz and I dance, I love kicking my feet high like a cheerleader and then shrinking to the floor and popping up again while turning in the air. Whether Liz laughs with me or at me while dancing in the way that works for her, the comfort we feel at home to be silly and imperfectly perfect makes our complacency level go down, and our excitement, happiness, and connection level go up.

Perhaps the sweetest moments are when immediately after that excitement, we connect with a romantic song such as John Legend's "All of Me," a song whose two words "perfect imperfections" remind me of our dancing and the type of love embedded in being each other's soul mate.

Creating Soul-Mate Gold: Game Playing

Most families play games with their kids but often forget to play games with each other. Almost all games create connection, but Liz and I find that rapid-movement games like foosball and Ping-Pong create the excitement of quick movement and quick points either won or lost, and a lot of laughter in the process.

For Liz and me, both still busy with our passion professions, foosball is ideal. We have a small foosball table that takes up almost no room and can be bought online for less than $30. We don't have room in our home for a Ping-Pong table, so we bought an outdoor weatherproof table that also works well for foursomes when we have guests.

Not to be outdone by their kids, some couples play video games such as *Guitar Hero* that allows you to be on the same team, enhancing cooperativeness, connection, and, well, a feeling of being on the same team.

For couples getting older (and which couples aren't!), a Japanese study found that just 10 minutes of Ping-Pong has the added benefit of increasing brain activity in the prefrontal cortex and cerebellum, and in the parietal, occipital, and temporal lobes. And that's just for starters. Nothing like having a brain enhancer as a love enhancer!

These forms of play are all love enhancers. But other forms of play, often ones inclusive of the kids, can be either love enhancers or love depleters. The difference emanates largely from the divergent interpretations by parents of the play's positive or negative influence on the kids. These include teasing, both with the kids and each other; roughhousing, especially with the kids; and sarcasm, especially with each other. Let's start with teasing.

Teasing: Teaching Emotional Intelligence Dad-Style?

Teasing is such a valuable art that in the past, jesters were employed by a king to tease the king. The king, who might kill someone who criticized him, paid for someone to give him the same criticism in the form of teasing. Today, though, some parents don't feel that way, especially if the teasing is directed at their children.

Tiffany, a mom of a boy and girl, volunteered, "The issue I selected for Caring and Sharing as the concern that would do the most to deepen our love if I felt fully heard by Jason is the way Jason teases our kids.

"The kids love playing with their dad, but Jason often teases them, and sometimes either Olivia or Jackson will break down crying. Especially Olivia. I shared with Jason how I couldn't believe that he doesn't learn from their crying and stop. How it made me afraid to leave them alone with him. Especially Olivia. What do you think, Warren?"

I hesitated. "I'll share some of my thoughts in a minute, but the important thing in this workshop is not what I think but that both of you feel

100 percent heard by the other and feel safe sharing all your feelings. Is that true for both of you?"

Both Jason and Tiffany nodded. "But we're still interested in your perspective," Tiffany added.

"Since you just did a Caring and Sharing about this, Tiffany, why don't you share what you heard Jason say?"

Tiffany and Jason shared a look-what-we-got-ourselves-into smile. Then Tiffany acquiesced. "Jason, what I heard you say is that you feel that I make it sound like the kids are crying all the time. But that in reality, the crying is rare—and they're over it in a few seconds and back to playing again. Besides, you say that people in the world make fun of you, and you have to know how to take it—even learn and grow from it."

Tiffany continued, "I did hear that point in Caring and Sharing, and am thinking about it, but I shared with Jason that I thought as parents we are supposed to protect our kids from bullies, not bully them ourselves."

"And what do you feel was Jason's perspective on that?"

Tiffany offered, "Jason, I heard you say that you feel that if you protect kids too much before they go out into the world by themselves, then you leave them unprotected when they go out into the world. Is that right, honey?"

Jason looked appreciatively at Tiffany for not doing a "but I feel that . . ." before he affirmed she had not distorted or missed anything. They hugged.

Jason then shared what he had heard Tiffany express. "I heard you say how terrible you feel when something we do as parents makes the kids cry—especially Olivia, who is so sensitive. I heard how you feel that our job is to keep them secure and loved, not insecure and bullied. You want me to stop the teasing because you want me to interact with the kids, and you think the kids benefit from me, so you don't want to feel you are being irresponsible when you leave the kids alone with me."

After Tiffany affirmed that nothing was distorted or missing, she looked at me with a now-we've-earned-our-answer playfulness. "OK, now what are *your* thoughts on this, Herr Doctor?"

"OK. First, teasing is an art form. If there's anger in Jason's voice, it's bad art: the anger takes over, and it's no longer teasing.

"When teasing is accompanied by a twinkle in the eye, indicating 'I'm on your team,' then **a parent playfully teasing a child is like a doctor inoculating a child: the vaccine 'teases' the child with a version of a real virus to help the child's immune system grow strong enough to fight off the virus in the real world.**"

"What's the virus?" Tiffany queried.

"The virus is criticism. Teasing's playfulness is to criticism what a fruit smoothie is to wheatgrass. The fruit smoothie allows us to get the benefit of the wheatgrass without the bad taste—it allows the wheatgrass to go down smoothly."

Tiffany, with a look of understanding yet with something still puzzling her, asked, "But I did try teasing Olivia once—in what I think was the same tone of voice that Jason uses, and she broke out crying almost immediately, and even more so than she does with Jason. How's that?"

"Olivia is used to mom language from you—you being more empathetic and serious than her dad is. In mom language, your teasing translates into serious criticism."

"Ahh. So how do I get her to respond to me more like she responds to Jason?"

"You may first try getting her buy-in by asking her if she likes it when dad teases her playfully, and if she'd like it if you played with her like that more often. If she buys in, that will give her a heads-up to be alert to your mom version of dad-teasing language. Fortunately, kids have remarkable abilities to learn new languages."

"Do you feel teasing will make the kids feel more loved?" Tiffany asked.

"From a nonteaser, it will feel like it's coming from anger, not love. But once the kids learn to interpret teasing as playfulness, the playfulness creates a bond with the child that, yes, increases love."

"Explain more about what they learn to interpret."

"It teaches them how to interpret the meaning of a twinkle in Jason's eye, slight alterations of his voice, shifts in his facial expression. **Teasing is a core component of teaching emotional intelligence.**"

Tiffany looked receptive. "Tell me more."

"Instead of teaching the children about red lights and green lights, teasing can offer Olivia and Jackson a way of understanding yellow lights. With a yellow light, you don't need to jam on your brakes, but you do need to pay more careful attention to a new series of nuances."

Another woman, Zoe, had been following all of this and looked captivated. She posed this challenge: "Bill and I both have kids from previous marriages, but they live separately. I'm having a lot of problems with my son—a teenager who, among other things, cares a lot more about playing video games than working on his homework. I'm always getting on his case with what he calls my lectures. How could I do it in your fruit smoothie way—by teasing?"

I paused, reaching for an example, then asked, "Is he interested in girls?"

"Oh yes."

"Well, since you have the credibility of being a woman, you might tease, 'Not to worry about your homework. Girls love dating losers.' But if you just stop there, it's half a tease and half a lecture. So add exaggeration. For example, you might say, 'I used to carry around this 20-foot sign in high school saying, Wanted: One Loser to Ask Me Out. No, just kidding. It was a 30-foot sign. No, it was . . . How big do *you* think the sign was?' That is, after your exaggeration, get him involved in exaggerating with you until you are both laughing together at its ridiculousness and at the image of you trying to carry, let's say, a 100-foot sign! When you're both laughing, you've created the fruit smoothie."

A bit overwhelmed, but also appreciative, Zoe smiled. "Wow, that *is* an art."

Zoe pursued, "So this exaggeration and laughter, which seems to come so naturally to guys, how do I learn this art?"

"If your husband does it well, watch him closely. And whether or not he does it well, also watch Steven Colbert, Bill Maher, *Saturday Night Live*, Jim Carrey, Dave Chappelle, Jon Stewart, Jerry Steinfeld, Johnny Carson, Robin Williams, or your favorite comedian. Start with Stephen Colbert's use of a raised eyebrow or the way he lowers his eyeglasses to create a caricature of someone. Observe how all the comedians switch voice tone, how they use the wink or roll of an eye, or hold a stare an extra second. Register how the longer they hold a stare, the greater the audience's laughter. If something by which you might otherwise have been offended is followed by that elongated stare or a raised eyebrow or a dropping of eyeglasses, soon your potential for being offended is trumped by your laughter."

Hearing all this seemed helpful to both Zoe and Tiffany. Tiffany put it succinctly. "I'm going to make an effort to learn this art, even if I don't master it like Jason has. Just realizing its value lets me see Jason as making a contribution rather than as being insensitive. So thank you."

I said, "Tiffany, you are fighting for Olivia and Jackson to be protected *now*. Jason is preparing the children to be protected in their *future*. The children need some of both. Both are virtues that when taken to the extreme become vices. That's why you both hearing each other's best intent and negotiating the best balance gives Olivia and Jackson the best of both your parenting styles—what I call checks-and-balance parenting."

Teasing in Marriage

Some studies find that married couples who tease each other during conflict feel more connected and happier after the conflict than those who criticize in a straightforward way.[3]

However, note that the choice here is twofold:

1. Raw criticism
2. Criticism in a smoothie of teasing so the conflict doesn't hurt as much as raw criticism would

Note that the studies just show that the teasing choice only *reduces the impact* of the conflict. The soul-mate choice gives you the opportunity to simultaneously *eliminate* the conflict and deepen your love while still being able to hear what is bothering your partner.

Teasing, Hazing, and Wit-Covered Put-Downs as Male Bonding

Bob, a man in his fifties, recalled, "I was in a fraternity at Florida State University. We were constantly teasing and hazing each other. Even when we went back for our twentieth reunion and I saw some of my frat brothers, we teased each other left and right. Angela was really confused since she had already heard me talk about these guys as being some of my best buddies."

"Yeah," Angela added. "Why do guys do that? I was in a sorority, and I don't do that with my sorority sisters. (Well, maybe a little, but nowhere near what Bob does.) Yet a few of them are among my best friends, with great memories."

I concurred. "Yes, the commerce of masculinity is trading wit-covered put-downs."

The workshop participants responded with snickers of both laughter and recognition. After I agreed to the requests of a few participants to repeat that, a woman queried, "Do guys have a reason for doing that, or is that just an example of toxic masculinity?"

After a few participants volunteered unabashedly, "toxic masculinity, duh…" and I pretended to concur as if there was nothing more to it, the air cleared and the participants created space for an alternative explanation.

"It creates male-style bonding. Even if your son's junior high school frowns upon it, your son will nevertheless experience it in junior high school. And he'll experience it even more intensely if he someday joins a fraternity.

"Fortunately, today he is much less likely to be bullied because schools are far more vigilant and punitive about bullying today than in the past. But instead of being bullied, if he's not respected enough to be teased, he'll be ignored. Being ignored is the new bullying."

"But why?" a young mom piped up. "It seems cruel and childish, and some of the fraternity hazing goes way too far. Fortunately, on many campuses it's being banned now."

Another woman smirked. "Men do it because they never grow up. You hit the nail on the head when you said 'childish.'"

After another laughter of concurrence—even among the men—died down, someone asked me if there was, in fact, any good reason for this "commerce of masculinity being the trading of wit-covered put-downs, or whatever you just said."

I paused to encourage a new focus. "Yes. boys' and men's trading of wit-covered put-downs has at least three purposes. First, boys' and men's trading of wit-covered put-downs is their unconscious way of preparing each other to handle the criticism it takes to become successful. (Try running for president if you can't handle put-downs!)

"Second, it prepares them to handle the criticism that comes after they become successful. (Try *being* president and not being able to handle put-downs!)

"And third, the teasing and wit-covered put-downs are a way of warning those brothers who become very successful to not get all puffed up with self-importance."

As I was letting this be taken in, a woman asked, "But if fraternity brothers are preparing to be future friends for life, why does their hazing sometimes purposely put each other in harm's way—that's not what you do to a friend. It makes no sense."

"The serious fraternity hazing—something to which I am strongly opposed—originated in a day when men bonded by proving they could make it as a man by demonstrating a willingness to be disposable. That was the male role: to prove his willingness to be disposable in war and disposable in the workplace. (To this day, 93 percent of the people who die on the job are men.) The serious fraternity hazing was men's way of preparing each other to be disposable in order to protect women, children, and the country, to be respected by parents and friends, and to be loved by the woman of their choice.

"For guys, the more hazardous the profession, the more its members bond by trading wit-covered put-downs. They're ubiquitous in what I call the death professions—the military, coal mining, construction, police, Alaskan crab fishing, and so on. For these men, a put-down isn't harassment; it's their diet. Women who rise in their ranks understand the meaning of their language."

"Can you give an example?" a woman asked.

"OK. For example, if a firefighter enters a burning building, he needs to know his partner will risk life and limb to save him. A partner who cannot be teased—who takes themselves too seriously, who is too thin-skinned, fragile, or narcissistic to laugh at themselves—also can't be trusted to risk his life to pull a partner out of the rubble after the ceiling collapses. So among guys, if you can't tease 'em, you can't trust 'em."

After pausing, I added, "Another example is in the armed services. By far the most hazardous is the Marine Corps. A marine knows that if he's wounded, a thin-skinned narcissist won't risk enemy fire to drag him to safety from where he was shot. Testing each other to see who is not just willing to die, but also strong enough to drag a fellow marine to safety creates a lifelong bond: 'once a marine, always a marine.'"

Since I was on a roll, I concluded, "Exactly because they have proved to each other that they are willing to be disposable, fraternity brothers often bond for life, sometimes becoming among the few long-lasting friends that men have. Fraternity brothers look forward to their fraternity reunions more than their college reunions.

"I say this because it is important to understand that historic purpose. But the future requires much more health intelligence. Bonding by proving your willingness to be disposable is heroic intelligence; it is not health intelligence. In fact, it is the opposite of health intelligence. Health intelligence involves giving yourself permission to feel your vulnerabilities and choose a friend in part based on your ability to trust that person to hear your fears and vulnerabilities.

"At its best, health intelligence incorporates some heroic intelligence— some of the discipline and postponed gratification it takes to tough it out— plus complete permission to be in touch with your feelings and choose friends who facilitate that. And for men, that vulnerability is a form of courage."

One of the women, more relaxed after she realized I wasn't advocating for heroic intelligence but explaining it, was still harboring a layer of doubt. "Isn't this hazing and teasing just another form of bullying?"

Her question inspired me to take the explanation to the next level. "Men tease and haze those they either respect or are testing to see if they are candidates for respect. Men bully those they don't respect. If a man stands up to hazing, he's respected and then he's earned being teased and hazed. Then he becomes part of the fraternity.

"Fraternity reunions are long planned and long anticipated. No one plans bully reunions."

Men Teasing Women at Work: Discrimination If He Does? Discrimination If He Doesn't?

One of the women in the workshop, who I found out later was a corporate director of Human Resources (HR), was intrigued. "If this trading of wit-covered put-downs and teasing, or hazing, or whatever, is men's way of preparing each other for success, is the fact that they just do it with each other a form of discrimination against women?"

She was a bit surprised when I answered, "Yes. If men at work confine their teasing to each other, it is in fact a form of discrimination against women."

"And that's why I have my HR job!" she exclaimed with a smile. "So what do we do about it?"

"The solution starts with understanding each other's best intent, just as we're doing with our partner."

"So what's men's best intent in confining their teasing to each other?"

"They fear that if they tease women, the women will see it as discrimination against women."

"So they feel damned if they do, and damned if they don't," the HR exec quickly surmised. "Can you give an example of what a guy might say to another guy that he'd be scared to say to a woman?"

"OK. A guy might go over to another guy at work who looks like he's gained a little weight, pat his belly, and shout out to the rest of their colleagues, 'Look everyone. John's pregnant.'

"He's afraid, though, that if he went over to a woman at work who looks like she's gained a little weight, pats her belly, and shouts, 'Look everyone. Jane's pregnant,' that Jane might file a complaint of discrimination with HR. The complaint might accuse that 'He came up and touched me on my belly—not even asking for my consent—and then mocked me in front of everyone for being fat. I was devastated. I couldn't concentrate for the rest of the week. This shows a complete lack of respect and is a clear case of both sexual harassment and workplace hostility. I don't feel either respected or accepted.'

"In groups of men unified either by physical danger (e.g., hazardous professions), significant responsibility (e.g., C-suites), or competition (e.g., team sports), teasing and wit-covered put-downs are not a sign of disrespect but a prerequisite to bonding. That is, to the guys, it is not a sign of rejection but acceptance.

"The weight gain or equivalent does point to a potential problem, but a guy will only tease about it with a guy he's gradually teased over time, a guy who has slowly been admitted to the club."

"Hence the old boys club," the HR director said with recognition.

"Yes, it's his boys club. No matter how much he may desire to admit women, he feels he can't even try out the admissions process on a female without jeopardizing his career."

"What's the purpose of this banter, teasing, and wit-covered put-downs in the workplace?" the HR executive pursued.

"In part, to create cohesion and much-needed relief from workday drudgery."

"So what's the solution to this sort of misunderstanding between men and women?" the HR executive's husband asked in a tone that suggested he and she had this discussion before.

"First, since women can't hear what men don't say, men need to translate their language to women at work during the hiring process. When the language is translated, some women will feel comfortable with it; some won't. They should know what they're getting into so they don't sign up for an uncomfortable situation.

"And second, once the women understand the male rationale, men need to ask the women to share what style of communication would make them happiest at work. Men also can't hear what women don't say."

"So you're saying that part of the HR process is women speaking up about what they need and want directly to the men?" the HR exec asked.

"Yes. Men need to hear that often, when women are the target of teasing, it simultaneously reinforces their feeling devalued and their beliefs that men are only paying lip service to equality."

"You're saying there needs to be a genuine dialogue sponsored by people like me as part of HR," the HR director both asked and summarized.

"Yes. We need to import the workplace equivalent of Caring and Sharing once a month or so at work. And that's best facilitated by HR."

Roughhousing: Dad as One More Child to Monitor?

After the workshop participants had completed the Caring and Sharing Practice, I asked them to share the one concern that if it were fully heard would do the most to deepen their love.

Jim confessed that "Lauren and I get into the most fights about my roughhousing with the kids. But I didn't bring it up because I don't quite know what to say to defend it—or whether I should even be defending it."

Checks and Balances Parenting: Mom-style parenting and Dad-style parenting

I looked at Lauren. "Lauren, what are your concerns about Jim roughhousing with the kids?"

"Basically that the kids will get hurt. And that's not just a worry. We have an eleven-year-old boy, a nine-year-old girl, and another boy who's six. More than once the roughhousing has ended with one of them getting hurt and crying.

"I feel like when Jim and the kids are roughhousing, I just have one more child to monitor. But since the kids seem to be having fun, and I don't want to be controlling or take away their dad time, I maybe give a tepid warning, but I try to back off."

"And then what?" I ask.

"Sooner or later one of the kids either gets hurt or starts crying. Then I feel guilty that I didn't pay attention to my intuition: my job is to protect the kids, and I failed. But at least I figure Jim will 'get it' that this is what happens, and he will either stop the roughhousing or not be so rough. But, no. He mutters something and then goes right back to the roughhousing until someone else ends up crying or getting hurt—and the cycle doesn't stop; he doesn't learn."

Lauren concluded, "*That's* why I feel like I have one more child to monitor!"

Several mothers in the workshop nodded in recognition, with one even applauding.

As Jim and a couple of the dads raised their hands to contribute another perspective, I asked Jim to first share what he heard Lauren say until Lauren said she felt that Jim had neither distorted nor missed anything. It took Jim a couple of rounds to rethink and restate those things Lauren felt were a distortion, but when Lauren gave him the now-I-really-feel-understood award, I felt a more relaxed and receptive energy from Lauren and the other moms. I then nodded to Jim to offer his perspective.

Jim was a bit nervous. "Well, first, the kids getting hurt has never, even once, involved any of the kids being seriously hurt. And only once was it to the point of little Jayden needing a Band-Aid. What the hurt is about is usually someone losing in the competition. Someone is pushed aside so they feel it is unfair, too rough, and cry."

"That's what I mean, too rough," Lauren interrupted.

I asked Lauren to do a Hold until she could find a mindset that would allow her to recenter herself and return to her state of receptivity.

Then Jim continued, "What I feel you are missing, Lauren, is that what you called *muttering* something and then returning to the rough-housing is me saying something like, 'Jackson, the way you pushed Jayden aside so forcefully and suddenly was too rough. You can use leverage, but if you push that hard again, there will be no more roughhousing tonight.'"

Lauren seemed receptive and relieved by the explanation until Jim got to "there will be no more roughhousing tonight." She started to interrupt with "Just tonight?" and then pulled back.

Jim picked up on Lauren's objection. "Yes, that's a consequence I can enforce. So if Jackson or one of the kids is too aggressive once again, I can just stop the roughhousing for the evening. Then the next time they beg me to roughhouse with them—some evening later in the week—and I remind them of the difference between what's acceptable and what isn't, they don't ignore me because they know that if they do, the roughhousing will end right then and there."

I reinforced what I felt was the key understanding: "Lauren, it's by actually stopping the roughhousing rather than just repeating the warnings that allows the kids to know that the next time they're too aggressive, they are going to lose the roughhousing rather than just hear another warning. That gives them the incentive to not err on the side of being too rough. That is, being too rough leads to 'winning' if the only consequence is a warning they can ignore; but being too rough leads to losing if they lose the roughhousing."

As Lauren shared what she heard Jim say along with my elaboration, she had a eureka moment. She looked at Jim. "Ah, I always get upset that when *you* tell the kids what they can and can't do, they seem to obey; yet when *I* tell them, they seem to ignore me. But I tend to just repeat my warnings. You stop the roughhousing, and the kids pay attention to you because they know you won't just repeat the warning ad infinitum like I do. They know they'll lose the roughhousing."

One of the moms in the workshop was frowning. "I question the whole idea of roughhousing to begin with. Isn't it just training for violence?"

Since I had done considerable research and thinking about this for my book *The Boy Crisis*, I was able to share the following insights. "No. Researchers consistently find that fathers who spend time with their children give their children the gifts of *self-control* and *social skills*.[4] When a dad—or mom—ends the roughhousing for the evening when it gets so rough that someone gets hurt or starts crying, they're teaching the difference between being assertive and being aggressive. This is a core social skill that they're teaching. They're teaching the children what psychologists call emotional intelligence under fire."

I decided to add a touch of nerdiness. "Studies of baby rats that engaged in rough-and-tumble activity find they become *less aggressive* and have more social skills as adults."[5] A lot of this is accomplished by the parent-child bond emanating from roughhousing—being 100 percent energized, laughing, spontaneous, and silly together.

While the bond is valuable in and of itself, it is also valuable for the leverage it creates for the parent: the parent can promise roughhousing as a reward for completing homework or a chore, or helping their brother or sister with a chore. And more important than the technical leverage is that the bond increases the children's desire to do what pleases the parent to whom they feel bonded.

The roughhousing bond that increases children's desire to work with rather than resist their parent is a lot like the bond created by feeling heard by our partner, which increases the desire we feel to work with rather than resist our partner.

Finally, probably the character trait we most desire for our children is the ability to empathize. A 26-year longitudinal study found that **the amount of time a father spends with a child is one of the strongest predictors of the child's ability to *empathize* in adulthood.**[6]

Roughhousing is one of the biggest differences between dad-style parenting and mom-style parenting, but there's nothing stopping a mom from adding roughhousing to her repertoire as a way to bond with her children and to develop her children's empathy by creating an incentive for them to be aware of their siblings' feelings.

Taken together, then, teasing and roughhousing can have counter-intuitive impacts of creating emotional intelligence and social skills—at least if the art of teasing is mastered, and roughhousing is coupled with boundary enforcement.

Sarcasm, though, is more complex and even more misunderstood than teasing and roughhousing.

Sarcasm

Among workshop participants in general (versus just the parents), sarcasm is perhaps the biggest telltale sign that a couple needs to move the issue to the Caring and Sharing Practice. However, while Caring and Sharing often leads to both partners feeling empathetic about their partner's feelings related to any given issue, it often fails to address the pain related to sarcasm. That's because it is rare for either partner to have the words to articulate what they were feeling that led them to be the giver of sarcasm, and how they felt when they were the receiver of sarcasm. So let's start there.

Some sarcasm is playful and not personal, such as raising one's eyebrows and commenting "I trust all politicians, don't *you*?" This type of sarcasm passes as humor (unless you're at dinner with politicians).

Sarcasm in the context of relationship conflict creates seldom understood problems for the receiver even as there is little understanding for what motivates the giver.

What the Receiver of Sarcasm Feels

Remember the Four-Part Apology given by Jacob to Emily in chapter 7? After Emily told Jacob, "You put the lightweight coat on Krista this morning, and she told me she was cold," Jacob responded in a loving tone, "I'm sorry. Yeah, I don't want Krista to catch a cold. I'll check the temperature more carefully in the future."

Imagine if instead Jacob had not responded with a Four-Part Apology but with this four-part sarcasm: "Oh yes. *You* always know exactly what to do. *I* care more about who's going to make the playoffs than about Krista. Let me know someday when I do something right, as if you'd even notice."

As the *receiver* of sarcasm, what is Emily likely to feel? Most likely, disrespected as well as the object of contempt, resulting in her feeling angry. And since anger is vulnerability's mask, yes, also vulnerable.

What the Giver of Sarcasm Feels

Most of us empathize with the feelings experienced by the receiver of sarcasm. However, few of us even contemplate the feelings experienced by the *giver* of sarcasm—including the giver of sarcasm!

Ironically, the giver of sarcasm is also likely experiencing a feeling of being disrespected, as well as the object of contempt stemming from a feeling of being repeatedly ignored ("Let me know someday when I do something right, *as if you'd even notice.*"). The result is also anger and the vulnerability hidden beneath the anger.

The difference is that the *receiver* of sarcasm often feels taken by surprise, as if suddenly hit by a bullet of anger, contempt, and disrespect.

The *giver* of sarcasm has often felt the anger, contempt, disrespect, and vulnerability accumulate *slowly*. When the giver of sarcasm doesn't feel safe discussing those feelings until they have experienced the Caring and Sharing Practice, the accumulation of anger, contempt, disrespect, and vulnerability build up until they erupt like a volcano, spitting out the hot lava—or bullets—of sarcasm that leaves the receiver scarred.

After I summarized this, one of my workshop participants, Nick, seemed to be holding back tears. "Yes, I feel like I say something repeatedly to Amanda, and she repeatedly ignores it. After a while, I feel like it's hopeless; like I don't matter. Like I'm chopped liver. And then, yes, I find myself becoming sarcastic. And for sure, the sarcasm is like me shouting to be heard. Maybe she'll pay attention to the 'bullet' if she won't pay attention to me."

I asked Nick and Amanda if either of them felt appreciated by the other. Amanda said, "When we first met, yes. But until yesterday [the first day of the "Role Mate to Soul Mate" workshop], neither Nick nor I had appreciated each other verbally probably for months. We say 'thanks for this' or 'thanks for that' but never at anything close to the five levels of specificity that we did with yesterday's appreciations."

Nick added, "And that grocery shopping example you gave of picking up 32 items and only mentioning the one that was wrong, well, Amanda and I are both guilty of that."

"Part of the damage, then," I offered, "is that you don't build up your reservoir of love, and therefore there is nothing to mitigate the feelings of not mattering and being treated like chopped liver."

Nick and Amanda both nodded.

When I was filming my online couples' course with two couples and discussing sarcasm and anger as vulnerability's mask, Annie said that her takeaway from that was to look for the *tears* behind the sarcasm. Her husband, Eben, added that in the future if he heard someone attacking him with sarcasm, he would inquire about the *loss of hope* beneath the mask of their sarcasm. Note that both the "tears behind the sarcasm" and the "loss of hope beneath the mask of sarcasm" reinforce our foundational soul-mate wisdom of anger is vulnerability's mask. Sarcasm is a form of anger. Sarcasm is also vulnerability's mask.

———

While it's easy to see how playing games and dancing with your partner can create soul-mate gold, there are other ways that people play—namely teasing and roughhousing with kids—that require a deeper understanding and a deft hand. Even whimsies in the style of Dave and Sharon have teasing elements. In this way, playfulness is an art, and it requires communication: what is playful to a Sharon may feel demeaning to a Dave.

As for couples who are all work and no play—you know, the ones who create a work-*work* balance—there is even more value from scheduling a fun night that involves active participation by both of them, be it a board game, Ping-Pong, or ballroom dancing.

Chapter 10

Secret 6: Creating Win-Win Solutions to Your Stickiest Problems

Remember how flexible you were when you first fell in love? How you were open to doing something you might otherwise never have considered? Your reservoir of love was full and you were receptive to experimenting with new versions of yourself that wouldn't disappoint your partner and often, in the process, even surprised yourself!

While long-lasting love has the gift of dependability, it often has the curse of complacency that dries up our creativity and the effort it takes to create win-win solutions without resistance to our partner's ideas.

If you wish to create win-win solutions to your stickiest problems, then it helps to emerge from complacency by making sure you have:

- Replenished your reservoir of love via a good Caring and Sharing Practice

- Shared multiple specific appreciations
- Maintained your Conflict-Free Zone

Creating Win-Win Solutions Step-by-Step

Step 1: Consider These Potential Decisions

- **Where should we live:** In a rural area, a suburb, a city, the mountains, or on the coast; in an inexpensive area or an expensive one with great schools; retire now or . . .
- **Vacations:** Exotic or local; camp, glamp, or Four Seasons; please both of us every time or rotate preference; expensive or put money into longer-lasting purchases; an experience in learning; health, relaxation, adventure, or exercise
- **Diet:** Vegan, vegetarian, meat; keto; avert diabetes; desserts; sodas and candy around the house; rotate preferences or please everyone; cooking separately; order in or eat out; weight loss?
- **Home maintenance:** What mess creates stress; dishes in the sink during the day or in the dishwasher right away; hire a housekeeper; repairs; home improvements that are necessary or that are cosmetic; protect against wildfires, floods, hurricanes; have insurance and generators for security or are they a waste of money
- **Career—money or meaning:** High-earning career or fulfilling lower-earning career
- **Do or study:** Start your own business and learn from experience or go for a business degree and learn in a classroom
- **Get married or live together:** If getting married, should you have a prenup; if living together, should there be a deadline for getting married
- **Her home, his home, a parent's home, or a new home:** Financial, psychological, or location considerations

- **Rent or buy:** If living together and only one can afford to buy; borrow to buy an additional home to rent to others in order to pay for primary home; time the market for optimal mortgage rates
- **Simplify or upgrade:** Work more and take out your maximum loan for your ideal home or simplify so you work less and have more free time
- **Children or no children:** If children, how many; biological or adopt; use in vitro fertilization
- **Parenting style:** Tough love or nurturing love; boundary setting or boundary enforcement; are roughhousing and teasing a positive or a negative; apply equality or equity to the children; styles of systematically negotiating checks-and-balance parenting; response to a child who feels she or he is gay or trans; ways to conduct family dinner nights so they don't become family dinner nightmares
- **Blended families:** Continue your old parenting styles or blend the best of both and be consistent with all the children; live close but separately, or live separately until the kids graduate high school—or hire a live-in therapist
- **Schooling:** Public, religious, boarding, Waldorf, Montessori, or homeschool
- **Vaccinating:** For ourselves, for our children; selected vaccinations, no vaccinations, or as many as possible
- **Spending or saving:** Enjoy money now or save for retirement; spend to invest; risk versus security
- **Children move back in:** Charge no rent, some rent, or market-level rent; chore sharing; deadline for moving out
- **Older parents:** Move in or move nearby; level of care and type of care
- **Loans:** Give a child, parent, or relative a loan; conditions for the loan; consequences if the loan is not repaid

- **Addictions:** (Addiction can be defined as any activity resulting in a negative outcome that would not have occurred if you had done less of it.) Decide what your stance is on gambling, drinking, overeating, porn, video games, dangerous sports, enabling your child, exceeding your budget; what to do when one of us strays into addiction territory

- **Sex:** Morning or evening; once a month or every day; traditional positions or experimental; if kids, when is sex OK and how do you explain it if they hear you; act out sexual fantasies or not; if your sexual desire gap is great, should you be monogamous or polyamorous, use pornography, see a therapist, take hormone therapy; is an affair the end, a symptom, the fault of the unfaithful, of both partners, or not a fault

A careful read of just the preceding examples makes it feel miraculous that any relationship survives! Especially those of couples with children and blended families.

Use the preceding 27 categories (that include about 200 decision possibilities) as prompts to express appreciations for the potential problems you have either solved, or never experienced. It's a good first step toward inspiring creativity toward win-win solutions.

Creating Your First Win-Win Solution: Exercise

The step-by-step process I outline in this chapter can be used whenever you and your partner need to reach consensus on a sticky problem. If you would like to do this as an exercise, as we do in the "Role Mate to Soul Mate" workshop, each partner should grab a notebook and do the following:

1. **Write down three problems** you feel would give you and your loved one the most benefit if creatively solved (see step 1 for inspiration).

2. **From among the three, choose the one problem** you feel would give you and your loved one the most benefit if creatively solved.

3. **Look at each other's first choice** and choose just one to work with. (Choose either one: You can always return to the other one in the future.)

Then proceed with the rest of the steps.

Step 2: Feelings First, Decision Second

The decision process after this step is rational, but our childhoods aren't. They are, of course, foundational. The more you and your partner share with each other these foundational feelings, the easier it will be for your partner to emotionally support you; they won't experience your different perspective as rejection, indifference, or criticism. And identifying the feelings emanating from those foundational experiences while simultaneously benefiting from the love and support of your partner will facilitate you letting go of those foundational experiences that are holding you back.

One caveat: Be aware of the potential for using these foundational experiences as an excuse to remain stuck. Pushing yourself to try something that you felt would aggravate those emotional roadblocks can often be helpful with letting them go (getting beyond them) as well as give you the courage to try something you thought you couldn't do in other areas. For example, if one of you was brought up a Roman Catholic and the other one a Buddhist, don't let your foundational emotional attachment to either religion prevent yourselves from going to each other's services together or watching a movie celebrating the Pope or the Buddha.

Therefore, before you contemplate the logistics of the decision, have a Caring and Sharing session on the underlying feelings that may influence you about the specific decision beyond what is technically rational. Some examples:

- If you are contemplating having children, use the Caring and Sharing Practice to share with your partner the values you absorbed as a child and any power they may have. Did your parents make it clear that anyone who didn't have children was selfish, or did your religious faith associate having children with godliness? Conversely, do you fear having children because your parents seemed to resent having had them because they felt they were never able to do what they really wanted, or you still feel traumatized by the alcoholism and domestic violence you feel emanated from their depression? Or have you always felt you could contribute more to the world than you could by having children?

- If you are facing a decision about your or your partner's parent moving into your home during a period of sickness, have your partner first create a safe space for your underlying feelings: Would you feel selfish and guilty if you didn't care for this parent? How do you feel about yourself when you spend a lot of time with that parent? How do you imagine it will affect you and your partner's relationship? How will it affect your career, and what are your dreams about your career that impact your identity? Conversely, do you feel that caring for this parent will help you heal a lifetime wound? Will you feel better about yourself for giving love to someone who has always given you love? Do you feel that it's just the right thing to do, and you will feel even more bonded with your partner if they support you through the process?

Step 3: Brainstorm Solutions—All Solutions

For this step, have a couple of notebooks on hand.

Sit across from each other. Take your partner's notepad and on top of a page, write your partner's name plus "Creative Solutions" (e.g., Tracy's Creative Solutions).

Approach the brainstorming as a sentence-completion exercise. Choose one of you to brainstorm first (the creative possibility creator) and one of you to transcribe. In rapid-fire mode, the person doing the brainstorming says, "One possible solution is" and then completes the sentence with a possible solution. The second that person finishes offering a possible solution, they repeat, "One possible solution is . . ."

Note: Laughter brings oxygen to the brain and increases creativity and receptivity. Therefore, the person doing the brainstorming should make the first possible solution a ridiculous one with the goal of making the two of you laugh.

The listener writes down everything, *whether or not it makes sense.* As the listener is fiercely scribbling, they need to be sure to frequently look at their partner with fascination, as if they were cheering their partner on, with *equal enthusiasm for every idea* without regard to judgment about the quality of the idea. The listener cheers, then, like a cheerleader would cheer. (A cheerleader doesn't say, "Hey, hey, what do you say, these two things were wrong with that play"!)

When the brainstormer feels they have run out of possible solutions, make one up. It will likely be impractical or inappropriate, but it will tap into the subconscious, often resulting in an idea that has outside-the-box creativity that could become practical with modification.

Step 4: Switch Roles

Repeat step 3, but this time the other partner is the creative possibility creator and the other the scribe. Yes, that includes coming up with a ridiculous opening joke/possibility again.

Step 5: Rate Your Partner's Possibilities

Both of you look at the other's list. Write a 10 next to what you feel are your partner's best ideas. Then a 9 next to the second best, then an 8, and finally a 7 next to the ideas you can at least live with. Don't put anything next to the remaining possibilities.

Step 6: Look at How Your Partner Rated Your Ideas

Take the pad listing your ideas (that your partner wrote down). Among the ones that already have a 7, 8, 9 or 10, mark your own number. If you feel an idea you had that is a 10 was ignored by your partner, write a 10 next to the idea and bring it up during step 7.

Step 7: Look at Both Lists Together

Start with any ideas that you both marked as 10 or 9. Discuss their possibilities. Work your way down to ideas you both marked as 7 or above.

Step 8: Choose a Solution and Make a Plan

If the problem being solved requires someone to stop a behavior (drinking, gambling, exceeding the budget) or accomplish something (lose ten pounds, exercise three times a week, cut back on sugar), create a reward or a consequence that increases the *incentive*. An *incremental* step toward a goal (e.g., losing five pounds) that starts with a small reward (e.g., sharing a favorite dessert—unless your goal was cutting back on sugar!) works best.

If you are disagreeing about solutions to the point of repeating your explanations of why your idea is better more than twice, or if either of you notices that you or your partner is raising their voice or has a tone of impatience or sarcasm, then schedule a Caring and Sharing time. Remember the Caring and Sharing Sandwich starts and ends with two specific appreciations.

Chapter 11

Secret 7: Creating Family Dinner Nights So They Don't Become Family Dinner Nightmares

wish my parents had taken this course. I would have been less screwed up," Sarah said, part lament and part self-deprecating humor.

"Then you wouldn't have married me!" Daniel pouted.

Samantha chimed in, "Well, *I* wish I had taken this course when I was a teenager. Instead of just arguing, I would have first told everyone 'What I heard you say…' and been the most popular kid in school!"

"Then you wouldn't be the humble woman I fell in love with," Megan lovingly countered as she hugged Samantha.

"Joking aside," Daniel continued, "Sarah and I have a nine-year-old daughter and a twelve-year-old son, and I don't think we can get them to go through the 24 steps of Caring and Sharing and all this discipline stuff. They just give us 'I'm fine'-type answers to 'Are you OK?'-type questions, but ten minutes later they're on the phone for an hour with a so-called BFF they hardly know. What's that about?"

I asked Daniel, "If your daughter says she's experimenting 'just a little' with drugs with this 'really great guy' she's met who attends the same church" what do you say?"

"OK, I get it. She knows we'd cross-examine her, as in 'Who's the guy,' and 'we don't care what church he's going to', and 'we don't care if it's just a little gummy that is legal in our state.' And so on. Ugh. The price of loving!"

"Don't they get it how much we love them and are just looking out for their best interests?" Sarah griped.

"Your love is to your kids like the ocean is to a fish—it's taken for granted. And the more your kids want the freedom to discover themselves by making their own mistakes, er, decisions, the more fearful they become of your power to restrict that discovery."

"Look at the upside," someone interrupted. "You've got power!"

Another parent argued, "But being a parent is not about power; it's about love. And if anything, the sacrifice of power—the sacrifice of time, money, flexibility."

"So with our kids, is there a solution?" Daniel pressed.

"Yes, but first the point about power is relevant. No one easily speaks truth to someone they feel has the power. And our kids haven't learned that there's rarely an absolute truth, as we saw in the exercise using the four pictures of Mario Cuomo: we all experience different pictures of the exact same event. Our picture is our truth. **When we're sure we have *the* truth, we rarely have truth; we usually have arrogance, self-righteousness and a closed mind.** Yet that's what's biologically natural for all of us—and certainly for our kids.

"So let's apply this to the solution of creating family dinner nights. Or more precisely, creating family dinner nights so they don't become family dinner nightmares.

"The goal here is twofold: First, to allow your kids to feel secure that they will be fully heard by you in the same way you now expect to be fully heard by your partner, even when you say something in Caring and Sharing that your partner may thoroughly disagree with.

"And second, to have your kids give that same gift to you, and their siblings. I'll be having you do this because when you only care for your children's needs, your children will be focused only on their needs."

I heard a questioning "huh" from a woman in the workshop.

I expanded. "That is, **if you give your children empathy but don't teach them to empathize, they don't become empathetic; they become self-centered.** Every family member must be heard, *and* every family member must practice making everyone in the family feel heard."

"That explains a lot," a teacher in the workshop piped up. "I have this self-centered kid in my class. On parent-teacher night I was unconsciously anticipating meeting self-centered parents. Instead, they were these empathetic, loving parents. Yet when I met the parents of this boy who was the most empathetic boy I've ever had, his parents were more the tough love type. Fascinating."

With that backdrop, here are six essentials for conducting family dinner nights (FDNs) so they don't become family dinner nightmares.

Essential 1: Timing

Your family dining together every night is ideal, but for this more structured FDN, once a week makes it a special occasion. Start with scheduling the same night each week. Each dinner should be scheduled for about one-and-a-half hours, but ask that no plans be made prior to two hours so no one feels cut off. If you don't complete the process below, decide among you whether to continue the following week or to schedule another FDN in the next night or two so no one feels left out.

Prior to the end of each dinner, review your schedules for the following week to see if the FDN evening needs to be shifted. Doing an *occasional* FDN without a particular family member is OK and sometimes instructive.

Essential 2: No Electronics or TV... Boundary Enforcement

Once the "no electronics" rule is made clear, electronics brought to the table on FDN are taken away for the rest of the evening. For multiple violations, multiple consequences.

Boundary enforcement is crucial here. A mom once told me, "I tell them 'no electronics at the table' but they hide them and look at them surreptitiously." When she said this as if she were helpless, I knew she had let her children become the parent when that served the children, and was the children's parent only to serve the children.

The mom objected that she had no leverage. When I asked what she and her husband did for the children, she acknowledged that they paid for all of their son and daughter's electronics, as well as for their favorite streaming services, video games, clothes, treats, and presents; that they drove their kids to their friends' homes, to movies and special events, often prepared a favorite dessert or favorite meal, and even cleaned up after their meals. The parents, as it turned out, had plenty of leverage, but were blind to it.

Why? The mom and the dad acknowledged that neither wanted to disappoint their children, and didn't want either child to cry or sulk. And they definitely wanted to avoid a possible tantrum. Sadly, they were both afraid of being disliked by their children.

Boundary enforcement is the most essential of the five essentials. If you're good enough at boundary setting, but weaker on boundary enforcement, do a careful read of the section on boundary enforcement on page 135 of *The Boy Crisis*.

Essential 3: Rotate Moderators and Ranges of Topics

Rotate moderators for each family dinner night from among the children mature enough to moderate. The moderator announces the topic of the night. If you have a child who is younger, they might make the topic whether they really have to be homeschooled—or go to a Catholic or a Montessori—school. Or why they have to get vaccinated when their friend's parents say vaccines hurt kids. Or why they can't play with their friend without their sister tagging along.

Topics may range from ones for which a parent moderator may wish input ("Should I take a job that will give us more money, but I'll have less time with you guys?"), to ones more broadly relevant to the family's life ("Is college necessary?" or "What should be the consequence of not doing an assigned chore?" or "Should the kids help with cooking?"), to dilemmas at school ("Is it better to do a variety of sports or specialize in one?" or "What should I do about a lonely kid in school who no one likes but I think is OK? If I hang out with him some of my friends won't want to hang out with me.").

Consider encouraging *role reversal*. For example, ask your child, "What would you do if you were a parent and your child didn't do their homework?" Role reversals are potent. You'll be amazed by your children's ability to share others' perspectives when you ask them to play out their role. You'll need to remind them to stay in the role; the longer they do, the more powerful the insights. Consistently doing role reversals can change the brain; practiced consistently at home, your children will find they begin to do it naturally at school and with friends.

Occasionally, topics can be more theoretical or controversial ("Is there really a God?" "Is abortion a women's choice, a woman-and-man's choice, or murder?" "Which political party is better for America?").

Essential 4: Make No Topic Taboo

Make the FDN more exciting than electronics. Kids—especially boys—love to be challenged and enter controversial territory. They'd rather only partially understand a conversation than be bored. And getting your daughter comfortable with controversy will encourage her to articulate her perspectives with less inhibition as well as to take risks. A willingness to take risks is one of the most important prerequisites for success.

Allow your kids a chance to experience human relations and family as more interesting than electronics by becoming comfortable facilitating a conversation in which everyone can feel safe expressing opposite opinions even on controversial topics. Part IV of this book, on Civil War to Civil Dialogue, will give you more practical ways to do this.

Essential 5: Check-ins, Then Timed Sharing of Opinions

Before discussing a topic, the moderator conducts a timed check-in (highlights of how you've been in the past week) of a max of three minutes per person. If someone has a serious problem, that takes priority for the night. If not, introduce the planned topic and, depending on family size, give each person between four and six minutes to share their perspective. No interruptions and no off-putting sighs or body language.

This is a good time to share with the family the picture of the four illustrations of Mario Cuomo (see chapter 6). Share how illustrator Thomas Fuchs imagined that Mario Cuomo, the former governor of New York, would be depicted by, clockwise from top left, Warhol, Picasso, Mondrian, and Robert Crumb. Each family member's story—*even of the same person or event at the same moment*—will often appear as different as these pictures.

There will be times when someone in the family is clearly not accurate. Imagine your six-year-old saying, "The sun rotates around the earth." Each family member's job is to listen fully—without interruption, sighs, smirks, dismissive body language or words, or mocking the speaker.

Essential 6: Use the What I Heard You Say/ Did I Distort Anything?/Did I Miss Anything? Process for Each Family Member

(See chapter 6, steps 4 through 6.) If your six-year-old is the one chosen to be fully heard that evening, then use this process before someone shares their response (e.g., why they believe the earth rotates around the sun). Remember that if the sharer says they feel sharing was distorted, then keep working on getting it right from their perspective, even if you think you got it right. In this context, the sharer is never wrong.

For perspective, as Carl Sagan put it in *Cosmos*, "Ptolemy's Earth-centered universe held sway for 1,500 years, a reminder that intellectual capacity is no guarantee against being dead wrong." That is, the most brilliant people in the world would have agreed with your six-year-old!

Part III

LIVING IN LOVE

Chapter 12

Creating Relational Feng Shui and Avoiding the Four Lazinesses

After I explained to my workshop participants that Liz and I light candles every night for dinner as part of creating our home's feng shui, a man in the workshop asked with a partially curious and partially smart-alecky smile, "Would you explain this 'fong shay'?" The group's laughter seemed to reflect a combination of shared curiosity repressed for fear of appearing ignorant, and amused condescension.

I shared that feng shui derives from Taoism, emanating from Chinese culture. It's a practice of arranging the items and furniture in rooms to create balance and bring about harmony between an individual and their environment. In this case, I was using the term loosely to refer to creating harmonious surroundings in our home with the idea of it contributing to a deepening of love.

"Well," Josh, another man in the workshop, intervened. "It seems that the feng shui in our home has changed, but not for the better."

I asked for an example.

"When Brittany moved into my home a couple of years ago, we had a move-in-together celebration. I gave her a beautifully wrapped box. In it was my garage door opener. As she removed it from the box, we both felt the pride and excitement of 'we did it.'"

"The next day when I returned from work, I could feel my heart pounding with excitement as the garage door opened and revealed Brittany's car. I knew that the moment we saw each other we'd be exploding with passion.

"But last week—just two years later—when I opened the garage door and it revealed Brittany's car, I found myself wishing that I had arrived first so I could have some alone time just to relax a little. I had zero anticipation of passion.

"Even though I still love Brittany—even more than when she first moved in—I hate it that I'm beginning to fantasize about other women. Do you think there is anything we can do to reignite the passion?"

Fortunately, the answer is yes. Let's look at three steps Josh and Brittany can take:

1. Altering Expectations
2. Reprogramming the Home's Feng Shui
3. Reevaluating the Choice-of-Home Decision

Altering Expectations

The initial passion is biologically natural. But our biological heritage protected us from the dysfunctions of long-lasting passion. Prior to birth control, if we continued to feel that passion every time we saw our partner, we'd be having more children than we could support financially. Even if we could have supported them, our level of exhaustion would have trumped passion!

Expectations of perpetual passion—expectations that are too high—reduce passion by making us disappointed in both us and our partner.

Step one, then, is mitigating the loss of passion by altering expectations.

The second step is exploring what Brittany and Josh can do to reignite *some* passion. I call it Farrell's Feng Shui (modestly, of course!).

Reprogramming the Home's Feng Shui

I asked Josh, "What is the experience you anticipate that makes you wish you had some alone time?"

"Oh, I don't know. Maybe it's coming through the door and immediately hearing, 'Oh, is that you Josh? Did you remember to pick up the dry cleaning?' or 'I started dinner thinking you'd be home sooner. Can you set the table and make a salad?' and then I look in the fridge and realize I had forgotten to pick up some tomatoes for the salad. Things like that."

In essence, when the garage door opened and Josh saw Brittany's car, it triggered Josh's visualization of a new set of responsibilities, expectations, and potential criticisms of unfulfilled expectations, with *minimal transition time from work responsibilities to home responsibilities.*

Is it possible for Josh to experience a different visualization that would be more likely to reignite passion than pressure? Yes, but to get there, we have to first look at what ignites passion.

Recall the last sexual relationship you had that was catalyzed by meeting someone with whom you felt strong chemistry but your flirtation was extended because you weren't sure whether your flirting partner shared your desire for a sexual relationship. *Finally*, one of you breaks through the fear-of-rejection barrier, and you connect physically. The passion is potent.

When desire is experienced with the possibility of acceptance dancing with the possibility of rejection, our heart throbs with passion. Passion is stimulated when desire encounters barriers to being fulfilled. If the barrier is too high, we give up; if the barrier is too low, the passion is less.

Going to a party, meeting someone new, and flirting without certainty of where it will go fits all those parameters. Josh and Brittany's two-year monogamous relationship fit none of those parameters.

What can Josh and Brittany do to simulate some of those parameters without forfeiting the security, trust, history, shared memories, and deepening bonds that can be among the upsides of monogamy?

They can try a version of the various forms of playing, dancing, teasing, and surprising each other that I detail in chapter 9, "Couples Who Play Together Stay Together."

Or try creating this feng shui…

Imagine the next time Josh pulls up to the garage and Brittany's car is revealed, he recalls Brittany having left a Post-it of appreciation in the refrigerator, on the leftover spaghetti and meatballs that he had made for their dinner the evening before. The Post-it reads,

Thank you for our dinner,
and especially this course:
the spaghetti, those meatballs (!)
and your marinara sauce.

Would the appreciation be too silly and the poetry too simple? Its silliness would doubtless have made Josh smile, and its simplicity would make it easy for Josh to remember.

The takeaway? Had Josh experienced this, there is a greater chance that the next time as he approached the garage, that memory would be triggered along with the *possibility* that something unexpected might just appear again this time.

Continuing this fanciful journey, imagine that as Josh sees Brittany's car that it also prompts another visualization, this one of the note Brittany had left a few nights before on the doorbell that he had fixed, again saying something silly yet appreciative, like:

Whenever you do
what I can't do well,
in my heart
it rings a bell.

Add a few more examples in different places around their home, and Brittany's appreciations would have, in essence, reprogrammed the house, catalyzing a reprogramming of Josh's visualizations.

This is a type of feng shui in the sense that this reprogramming is balancing the everyday expectation of responsibilities with the anticipation of surprise no matter where in the house Josh walks, affecting the balance of energies in their home.

Of course, this practice of, er . . . "Farrell's Feng Shui" is a two-person game. Josh, too, can do things to create a similar experience for Brittany. Maybe while Brittany is showering and the mirror is steaming up, he'll trace into the steam, "You steam up more than this mirror." Or he puts a note in her left shoe with the question "Will you be my soul mate?" and in her right shoe a note saying, "My soul mate awaits your answer." Again, it's silly; it's simple, and therefore memorable.

Josh now anticipates Brittany being surprised but does not know when she will discover her surprise. He anticipates that leaving Brittany a note once might inspire a visualization on Brittany's part of other possible surprises when the garage door opens and his car is revealed.

The parameters of this reprogramming, the anticipation of the possibility of something both new and positive but with no guarantee, contain the potential for igniting passion.

Understand, we're not talking about the passion of Josh and Brittany's first encounters but considerably more passion than complacency provides.

Reevaluating the Choice-of-Home Decision

Making sure that both of you are reflected in your home's décor and furniture is an important component of relationship feng shui. If one of you has a much more limited budget, then use estate sales or consignment shops to bring each of your personalities into the home at an affordable price.

However, there's a much bigger issue: one person moving into the other's home. Even if that makes financial sense, it almost always challenges the relationship's feng shui. Josh and Brittany shared with the group exactly how.

Josh started. "Well, I own my home, and Brittany was renting hers, so we thought we would save Brittany some rent (she's paying me something, but quite a bit less than she would be paying for the house she was renting). Brittany said she liked my home, so it seemed like a win-win. But it became a lot more complicated than that."

I asked, "Would you both give me a few examples of those complications? Maybe Brittany, you start?"

"Yeah. Josh has everything the way he likes it: from bamboo sheets and pillow cases, whereas I prefer Egyptian cotton, to bedspreads that don't match the paint in the room, to a boring paint job, to weights that make the bedroom look half like a gym. And I guess what bothers me the most is sleeping with him every night in a bed that for him had memories of who knows how many other women! And that's just for the bedroom.

"You should see the way he has the kitchen set up! I feel I have to fight for every suggestion that I make. I feel like a visitor, not a partner; as if I'm always asking 'Daddy' for permission. I feel more like a child than an equal. It sure doesn't turn me on."

Josh responded, "I can see how it must feel like that to Brittany, and we're going to bring this up in the Creating Win-Win Solutions session once we do a good Caring and Sharing about it. However, my feelings are sort of a parallel opposite. Exactly because my home reflects *me*, I feel it is me who is constantly being torn apart and criticized: saying the towels are cheap feels like Brittany's saying I'm cheap, even like I'm not the quality of man who is good enough for her. Brittany likes my muscles but hates my weights. I feel picked apart and controlled.

"All the focus is on what Brittany doesn't like, not on anything she likes. And there's never any gratitude for saving her more than $10,000 a year in rent. And it doesn't stop with the bedroom or kitchen, but 'the garden has too many weeds; it needs to be landscaped. It needs more flowers, and we should have a Japanese maple tree.' Why not just landscape me!" Josh exclaimed, smiling at his frustrated exaggeration. "What do we do, Doc?"

"Your resolution to start with a Caring and Sharing session and then move on to the Creating Win-Win Solutions exercise is perfect. As you hear each other, you will be able to come up with dozens of other examples exactly like those you just mentioned. And that is what tears apart— and often plants the seeds of destruction—almost every relationship in which one person moves into the home of the other."

"Based on what you've heard from other couples in our situation, would you suggest we give priority to one or two approaches that have worked for other couples?" Brittany queried.

"Perhaps check out creative win-win possibilities of finding a home you choose together, with a design, price, and location that you can both agree on. And do the best you can to decorate it from scratch, and either furnishing it from scratch or adding about an equal amount of furniture from your past. Perhaps explore the possibility of a new bed."

Brittany asked, "What about if Josh has a lot more money than I do?"

"Overall, work that out in Caring and Sharing and Win-Win Solutions. Consider options such as becoming a one-third or one-quarter owner. Or the possibility of bringing in a third owner who doesn't live in the home but you all agree they receive a percentage of the increase in the home's price when you sell it or at some other point in the future.

"There are too many variables to impose one formula, but, as a rule, err on the side of both of you being owners *even if it means downsizing.*

"And keep in mind that most people stay at a location longer than they had predicted. If you are planning to have children, or your children will be leaving the nest in more than five to eight years, incorporate more long-term considerations than you might otherwise be inclined to do."

At this point a man in the workshop, Frank, shared an important experience he was enduring.

"In our case, Mary owned her own home, I rented mine, and I moved into her home. We experienced everything you've all been talking about, but I feel like the child, and I often feel Mary sees me that way—or at least like less than equal.

"And I also feel something else is transpiring, like the fact that I don't also own a home makes Mary feel less respect for me. At worst, I sometimes feel that she wonders if I might be using her. I say that because she tells me that's what a couple of her women friends have cautioned. All this makes me feel like she has less respect for me than I would like. And as you've said earlier in the workshop, it's very hard for a woman to love a man she doesn't respect."

Mary shook her head in tacit acknowledgment.

I confirmed, "Yes, when a man who doesn't own a home moves into the home of a woman who does, the problems faced by Josh and Brittany are very likely to be compounded by exactly the problems you and Mary are experiencing."

Mary got involved. "What would you suggest?"

"Well, first, with something as crucial as respect, begin with specific appreciations of what you respect about each other.

"Second, do an appreciation evening based on the wisdom that the choice of our partner is our most important statement as to the choice of our values (chapter 3, Wisdom #2). What did you value that led you and Frank to choose each other?

"Third, give yourselves the expectation of doing multiple Caring and Sharing sessions on this topic, and a lot of attention to creating win-win solutions.

"And don't give up. Together these processes will add to your relational feng shui. **The tougher the decision is that you successfully navigate, the more your love will deepen.**"

———

Since virtually everything that works to sustain love is unnatural, it is inevitable that with all of life's other demands, you'll often resort to what is natural but less functional for sustaining love. For reasons that follow, some couples who are unaware of these Lazinesses can have their worst fights.

Avoiding the Four Lazinesses and One of Your Worst Fights

On one of my postworkshop group follow-up Zoom calls, a woman named Stephanie lamented, "Amanda and I had such a great workshop experience, but it only lasted about six weeks. And then the night before last we had one of the worst fights of our seven-year relationship.

"We've tried everything, and this seemed to be the one thing that worked—until it didn't. Warren, we're thinking about breaking up. Amanda and I both agree that it seems like we're just not meant for each other."

I asked Stephanie and Amanda, "Do you always have a date for your Caring and Sharing on the calendar, and if you do, are you in fact doing it?

"Well, we were doing really well the first four weeks, but then Amanda went on a business trip, and although we planned to do it by Zoom, Amanda was jet lagged, so we put it off. We never got one back on the calendar."

"Did you maintain the Conflict-Free Zone?" I queried.

Stephanie said, "Mostly. And it helped a lot. But we got sloppier after Amanda returned from her trip. Nothing came close to last Friday night, when Amanda said I was leaving too many things around the house. I shot back that she was OCD. Then she labeled me Sloppy Steph. I called her boring. You don't want to hear where it went from there!"

"Got it. Did either of you say 'Hold'?"

"Ha!!" They both laughed/cried.

"OK," I offered, "I have some good news for you. Virtually every time a couple has had one of their worst fights after a workshop, it is almost always after the workshop has worked well for them for a while, and then between one and four of the Four Lazinesses are committed—the ones I discussed in the workshop."

"Oh yes." They both nodded. It seemed like they had but a faint recollection.

Amanda recalled, "Yeah, we did a Caring and Sharing, and it worked well. But then we stopped. I guess that was one of our lazinesses, right?

"You got it. Stephanie, can you pinpoint another?

"Well, we for sure violated the Conflict-Free Zone by just dropping bombs on each other until we both exploded."

Then someone else on the call added, "And obviously, neither said 'Hold'—wasn't that another laziness you brought up in the workshop?"

"Good," I affirmed. "And the fourth laziness?"

Stephanie took a best guess. "Something about the mindsets?"

"Yes, giving short shrift to the Six Mindsets."

"We were pretty good about that until we stopped doing a Caring and Sharing in the last few weeks."

"Then you *really* gave short shrift to the mindsets—by not doing them!" I teased.

"Any recollection as to why couples have one of the *worst* fights when, after all, prior to taking the workshop you never even knew about the Four Lazinesses? Why wouldn't you have had one of your worst fights when you had not done any of those things?"

Amanda volunteered, "Because we've taken off our armor and feel more vulnerable. And as you say, anger is vulnerability's mask."

"Great, that's exactly right. Let me dig a little deeper. Taken together, the Art and Discipline of Love deepens your trust and love and increases your expectations of feeling heard. The longer you do these practices, the deeper the trust and love and the greater the expectation that you will be heard. So gradually some—and potentially virtually all—of our armor is removed.

"Then one day when you've committed one or more of these Four Lazinesses and your partner shares a concern, you hear it as a criticism. Your partner, in a normal state—not the altered state created by the Six Mindsets—feels more vulnerable than ever and responds with more anger than ever. You have the worst fight ever.

"Your false conclusion is that you've tried everything and you're worse than ever; you're not meant for each other.

"However, there is a more love-enhancing conclusion: *The process worked. It deepened our love. And therefore, it deepened our vulnerability.*

"The solution: Return to the Art and Discipline of Love. Avoid the Four Lazinesses. Remember that falling in love is biologically natural; sustaining love is biologically unnatural. Sustaining love requires the unnatural discipline that you temporarily forgot.

"So, Stephanie and Amanda, here's my conclusion: You're human. Try again. Avoid the Four Lazinesses and rediscover your trust and love."

"Wow. Thanks. OK, Steph, I'm on board. You?"

"Yes. I hate that discipline stuff. But I love Amanda more!"

Why the Four Lazinesses May Lead to Your Worst Fight Ever

1. The Art and Discipline of Love deepens your trust and love.
2. This raises your expectations of being heard, allowing you to remove your armor.
3. So now, if you are not heard, you feel betrayed. And without armor, you feel more vulnerable.

Anger is vulnerability's mask.

Three Steps to Turn the Worst Fight Ever into Your Deepest Love Ever

1. Eliminate the Four Lazinesses
2. Practice the methods of sustaining a Conflict-Free Zone
3. Do a Caring and Sharing Practice and don't forget the specific appreciations at the beginning and end (the Caring and Sharing Sandwich)

Chapter 13

Committing to Change and Renewing Your Vows

This chapter prepares you and your partner to make a commitment to change a behavior, an attitude, or both, followed by either a renewal of vows or a creation of vows that incorporates some of what has been most meaningful to you from the *Role Mate to Soul Mate* book and online video course (see the Appendix for the QR code).

You'll need four pieces of 8½" × 11" solid white paper for each of you, and a total of four or five crayons of your favorite colors.

Solo Exercise #1: Panning for Gold

Hopefully, you've been practicing panning for your partner's gold throughout the book and online course, so this should be easy.

Write down three appreciations of your partner based solely on what you've observed about your partner since you started the course. These three appreciations should be something new; something you have not already shared with your partner while doing the exercises in the book or following along with the online workshop. Leave space to incorporate four to five levels of specificity.

When I gave this instruction in one of my workshops, a man raised his hand and said, "Man, I think I've covered everything; I've probably done more appreciating of Cindy this weekend than I've done since we've been married. (Well, maybe since after our honeymoon!) Any suggestions, Doc?"

I asked the workshop participants for ideas.

Vicky started, "I appreciate the way Gary packed our luggage into the car this morning so we wouldn't violate the checkout time."

"Great. Now come up with a specific and speak directly to Gary."

"Oh boy. Let's see. Gary, I appreciate that you did that without my asking."

"Good. Another specific?"

"Um, I appreciate you knowing that I get stressed when I have to rush through meals preoccupied with another obligation, like the pressure of having to pack the bags before checkout time."

"Great. Another?"

"Ugh. Let's see. OK, you know that I've been dealing with some back problems, so you lifted even my large, heavy suitcase into our small trunk without saying a word, probably so I wouldn't feel guilty not helping."

"Yes! One more specific?"

"You never give up, do you?" she laughed. "OK. I appreciate how you found out when we needed to check out, packed your own bags first, and gave me more time to complete my own packing, knowing that we're going from here to my niece's wedding, and I want to be sure things aren't wrinkled."

As I began to acknowledge her, one guy objected. "These appreciations are filled with assumptions that he did all these things consciously. How does she know that?"

I looked at Gary. "Gary, if you get credit for doing something consciously that maybe was only half conscious or maybe even just a coincidence, how do you feel about that?"

"OK, point made. Yes, any appreciation of me by Vicky is not going to undergo an intellectual analysis!"

Laughter, and even some applause signaled that everyone got it.

I concurred. "For your specifics, coming up with assumptions about your partner's best intent is not only permissible, but encouraged. When we think our best intent has a chance of being discovered, we become more motivated to actively look for what we can do that our partner will discover and appreciate. In brief, the mere search for our partner's best possible intent—whether technically accurate or not—crystallizes our love. It works as the opposite of complacency."

Solo Exercise #2: Appreciation Solidification

1. Review *all* the appreciations that you've shared with your partner thus far as you've worked through the exercises in this book or by watching the online workshop (see Appendix for QR code).
2. Look carefully at the specifics. Choose the top five or six. They will be used in this exercise to help you appreciate your partner even more than you did prior to reading this book or watching the online workshop.

Keep these to yourself for now; you will incorporate them into your renewal of vows.

Solo Exercise #3: Embedding the Best Ideas into Your Memory

Decades ago whenever I had what I thought was a great idea in the shower, I'd promise myself that I would write it down as soon as I got out. I usually discovered that by the time I dried off and located a pen, I had already forgotten the most creative of the ideas. (And that was when I was younger!) It seemed like the more creative the idea, the more quickly I forgot it! Why? If you've ever listened to a memory expert, you learned to associate what you wish to remember with something you already know. That is, give it context.

However, **the more creative an idea is, the less context it has, therefore, the faster we forget it.**

The best and most creative ideas require repetition. If you ask someone if they heard a good joke lately, they may well say yes. When you ask them to tell you the joke, they are likely to either not be able to recall it, or awkwardly stumble through it. A professional comedian solves that problem by repeating a joke three or four times shortly after first creating it. That's what this exercise will help you do.

Review all the chapters, noting what you underlined or starred as well as your personal notes from the book or online course. Write down the seven ideas that would have the most value if you were able to integrate them into your everyday life.

1. Be very specific (e.g., not "I loved the mindsets" but "the Die for Partner mindset helped me most").
2. Write why the idea has the most value.
3. Then write how you will integrate the idea in your everyday life.

Interactive Exercise: Insight Sharing Game

To embed your most important insights into your foundational wisdom:

1. Select your top four insights or takeaways.
2. Rotate sharing these insights or takeaways with your partner until you both share three.
3. If your partner is the first to share a takeaway that's on your list, mention that you also chose that one, then choose one that has not yet been shared.

Interactive Exercise: "What I understand or appreciate about you better than before is ..."

1. Mentally review your appreciations from Solo Exercise #1, "Panning for Gold," and Solo Exercise #2, "Appreciation Solidification."

2. Sit face-to-face with your partner, making eye contact.

3. Choose one of you to begin; the other to soak it in.

4. You'll be doing a sentence-completion exercise by repeatedly saying, "What I understand or appreciate about you better than before is ...," and completing the sentence differently each time.

5. For example, "I understand and appreciate how your teasing the kids is a way of preparing them for emotional intelligence and resilience." Or "I understand and appreciate better than before how putting the dishes directly into the dishwasher rather than in the sink gives you a sense of peacefulness and a feeling of being more respected." Share at least a half dozen.

Commitments to Change

Choose one or two specific commitments to change, such as:

- "I commit to doing a Caring and Sharing session every Sunday morning."

- "I commit to always having a Caring and Sharing session on the calendar."

- "I commit to treating your biological children from your former marriage with the same attentiveness as I do my biological children."

- "I commit to going on whatever vacation you choose every other year, knowing that you will go on whatever vacation I choose on the alternate years (as long as our health is not in jeopardy)."

Write out the commitment artistically on one of your sheets of white paper. Use crayons, a Sharpie, colored pencil, etc.

Sign and date it.

Do not show this to your partner until the renewal or creation of vows ceremony.

Renewal or Creation of Vows

Your renewal or creation of vows can be poetic and vision-oriented, but keep it specific and honest—not more than you can deliver. For example, it is doubtless more than you can deliver to say, "I vow to *always* listen fully and *never* be defensive," but "From this day forward I vow to devote more of my time, energy, and focus to care for you and the children than I have ever done before" is likely to be more viable and therefore honest.

Write out your renewal or creation of vows artistically on one of your sheets of white paper. Add some color. Sign and date it.

Do not show this to your partner until the renewal or creation of vows ceremony.

Closing Ceremony

Gather together your questionnaire on your style of defensiveness, your committing to change solo exercise #1, and your renewal or creation of vows.

Play your most romance-inspiring orchestral or piano/harp-type music, such as Pachelbel's Canon in D Major (the one I use in my workshops). Then follow these steps:

1. **Eye contact:** Stand across from each other for about a minute, focusing on both the eye contact and the music to deepen your connection.

2. **Rip up the questionnaire on your style of defensiveness (from chapter 4):** Do this only if you feel committed to employing the methods of sustaining a Conflict-Free Zone (e.g., journaling), reviewing the book and online video course after about six months, minimizing the Four Lazinesses, and trying again with gentle forgiveness of yourself and your partner when either of you is less than perfect. Say that to your partner in your own words and then *rip up* the questionnaire into small pieces, and give the pieces to your partner.

3. **Commitment to change:** Read your commitment to change to your partner. If there is anything especially meaningful about the way you created it artistically, share that with your partner. Then give the piece of paper to your partner.

4. **Renewal or creation of vows:** Read your renewal or creation of vows to your partner. Again, if there is anything especially meaningful about the way you created it artistically, share that with your partner. Then give the piece of paper to your partner.

5. **Framing:** Consider framing your and your loved one's renewal or creation of vows and commitments to change and hanging them in your bedroom.

6. **Reward yourselves:** You've just completed an evolutionary shift in the way humans evolved to communicate. Give each other a huge hug and celebrate!

Part IV

FROM CIVIL WAR
TO CIVIL DIALOGUE

Chapter 14

Applying Soul-Mate Consciousness to Family, Friends, Colleagues, and, Yes, Political Opponents!

I t is likely you started this book thinking that when you got into an argument, you were right—otherwise you wouldn't be arguing! Hopefully, two things are now apparent: first, you don't know if you are right if you only know your perspective; and second, once you've heard your partner's perspective, it's often apparent that either you're both right or you're both right and wrong or there really is no right or wrong—*you were both looking at the world through different life experiences that contributed to the very reason you selected your partner!*

In "From Civil War to Civil Dialogue," we'll apply what we learned to do with our loved one—provide a safe environment for their criticisms, concerns, and possibly never-to-be-agreed-upon perspectives on any given issue—to the rest of the world. The difference? Virtually no one in the rest of the world has viewed or read *Role Mate to Soul Mate*.

Since you and your partner are virtually alone in creating this evolutionary shift, I'll be teaching you how to modify what you've learned to do with your partner for everyone else in your life. This is what I call "Alone Power."

> For updates on the real-world implementation of "Civil War to Civil Dialogue," check the Couples' Communication tab on my website (warrenfarrell.com).

Alone Power

When you learned to sustain the Conflict-Free Zone (chapter 7), you learned the core of Alone Power. I shared that the moment you receive criticism, you can visualize your response to be something like, "I think I'll be able to listen to you better in Caring and Sharing." Thus, the criticism won't escalate into conflict.

Once you learned that, you implicitly learned that any fight that escalates is whose fault? Correct: you're both at fault. Now you know who to blame!

Let's apply this to Alone Power for the rest of the world—because with anyone else, you won't be able to wait for a formal Caring and Sharing session to work through your issue. Alone Power is the ability for you, alone, to leave everyone you encounter feeling heard. At its core, Alone Power is a one-way form of a Caring and Sharing session. It is a method of modifying soul mate–type consciousness so it can be applied to family, friends, colleagues, and political opponents. And even when a family member, friend, or colleague is that political opponent, you will learn how to use Alone Power to turn your potential civil war into a civil dialogue.

To implement Alone Power, you'll learn about:

1. The mindsets that create Alone Power
2. Applying Alone Power to your family regarding personal issues (e.g., "Mom and Dad always favored you.")
3. Applying Alone Power to friends (e.g., "We have your kids over for playdates, but you rarely reciprocate.") or colleagues (e.g., "How is it that you work from home in your pj's whereas I have to commute an hour each way, but you still get the same pay?")
4. Applying Alone Power to family, friends, and colleagues who have different political perspectives (No examples necessary!)

The Mindsets That Create Alone Power

Similar to the Six Mindsets of Receptivity in the Caring and Sharing Practice, these thought exercises will help you get into the right frame of mind for Alone Power.

The Nemesis Visualization

Close your eyes for a moment. Visualize a person in your life who listened to you just enough to misunderstand you, interrupt you, argue with a distorted version of what you said, tell you what they "know" is right, and then kept repeating their version with no interest in your input. Let's call this person your nemesis.

Continue visualizing.

Say to yourself that *since this person has not taken the course, I will lower my expectations: I may get a chance to respond, but I won't expect it. I won't even fantasize it!*

What, though, is the purpose of even caring about your nemesis?

If your nemesis is a colleague or family member, recall their need to repeat themselves and argue. The more you master Alone Power, the more you'll notice that **by leaving them feeling heard, you've left them with nothing to argue about.** The safety they feel with you listening and the freedom they feel when they speak to you softens their attitude toward you.

Let's dig deeper.

People who repeat themselves and argue are usually insecure and emotionally starved. **Your listening will allow an emotionally starved person the rare experience of feeling emotionally replenished.** You become the rare someone in their life who isn't self-listening while they are talking. The worse they are, the better you'll make them feel.

If they are a colleague, visualize how often other colleagues are likely to have ignored them, tuned out, or even avoided them. As they begin to repeat their self-destructive ways, they experience what might be thought of as a type of PTSD.

When you do this one-way Caring and Sharing, they'll feel more peaceful when they share, which will increase their respect for you and allow themselves to begin to care about you.

If they are a family member, imagine them feeling more loved, respected, and cherished. What could be a more soul-enhancing gift?

The Visualization for Everyone—Nemesis or Not

Visualize using these steps from the Caring and Sharing Practice:

1. Hear what they are saying with curiosity and without interruption.
2. Share what you feel you heard them say and then ask if they feel you distorted anything. Recall how in a Caring and Sharing session, if your partner felt you distorted anything, whether

you agreed or not, you nevertheless kept working at it until your partner felt nothing was distorted. Visualize doing this even with your nemesis.

3. Ask if they feel you missed anything. As with the distortion question, you keep working at it until your nemesis feels nothing was missed.

Visualization complete.

Alone Power with a Family Member about Personal Issues

If you experience a member of your immediate or extended family as either your nemesis or merely someone with whom you experience a lot of tension, prepare before you make contact by doing visualization and then reviewing this modified version of the Six Mindsets you learned in chapter 6, "The Caring and Sharing Practice." Eliminate the Die for Partner mindset unless the family member is someone you would risk your life for despite the tension (e.g., your son or daughter). Use the following five mindsets:

1. **Love Guarantee:** The more I provide a safe space for my sibling's/parent's/child's feelings, the more they will feel loved by me and the more they will feel more love for me.

2. **Cinematic Immersion:** First, if I feel myself getting upset, I'll tell myself that it's only a movie. Since neither my sibling/parent/ child nor a movie are physically hitting me, I can relax.

   Second, I'll remind myself that at a movie I don't argue with the actors' stories—I immerse myself in the actors' stories. I don't leave early; I stay to the end.

173

I can relax and immerse myself in my sibling's/parent's/child's story to the end.

3. **Attach/Detach.** I cannot attach to my sibling's/parent's/child's story until I detach from my defenses, defenses like "I have a response to that."

    If I can't stop myself from self-listening, I will tell myself Hold and recall either another mindset or part of the visualization I just practiced.

4. **Stream:** If I feel my sibling/parent/child is distorting or angry, I will visualize that as pollution in a stream. I will imagine my listening as being a filter, filtering out those impurities.

5. **Eye Contact:** Only after I have altered my naturally defensive mindset can my eye contact be genuinely supportive because I feel safe, and therefore my sibling/parent/child is safe, and our love will deepen.

    If you haven't done the preparation ahead of time and you're taken off guard in the moment, tell yourself Hold until you've recalled a mindset or two that works best to recenter you.

Alone Power with a Friend or Colleague

With a friend or colleague who is a nemesis of sorts, review ahead of time the nemesis visualization, plus these five modified mindsets:

1. **Respect Guarantee:** The more I provide a safe space for my friend's/colleague's feelings, the more they will feel respected *by* me, and the more they will feel more respect *for* me.

    Then review:

2. **Cinematic Immersion**

3. **Attach/Detach**

4. **Stream**
5. **Eye Contact**

Again, if you haven't done the preparation ahead of time and you're taken off guard in the moment, tell yourself "Hold" until you've recalled a mindset or two that works best to recenter yourself.

Alone Power with Political Opponents

In both the US and globally, most people yearn for their country to be more united. But when pressed, the unification wish rarely starts with, "I need to make more of an effort to find the best intent of the people with whom I disagree." The desire for unification often amounts to a desire for everyone to understand the value of our own perspective.

Our crisis of divisiveness is in part a crisis of closed-mindedness. The degree to which we're quite certain we've thought things through and come to the only correct answer really is the degree to which it is a crisis of self-righteousness.

How bad has this gotten? Only about half of US college students expected to graduate in 2025 would even be willing to be a *roommate* with someone who supported their opposing 2020 presidential candidate (according to a 2022 NBC News/Generation Lab survey). This spills over to family gatherings and office settings in which everyone agrees on only one thing: "We should all be better listeners. Here's my perspective."

The Detective-Therapist Visualization

When it appears like you will soon be listening to your political nemesis, start with the Detective-Therapist Visualization: the one I introduced in chapter 6 as either an alternative or an addition to the Six Mindsets.

Visualize:

"I am a detective searching for every piece of your puzzle until I see your full picture. To discover every piece, I must be curious. I will keep drawing you out until you are thinking thoughts you didn't even know you were thinking. My goal? To see your whole picture as clearly as you see it. My litmus test? When I've got the puzzle right, I'll see why your picture looks the way it does. Then I can genuinely say, 'Now I see how that makes sense [to you].'"

When a detective pieces together the puzzle, it's usually to prosecute. When you use Alone Power with your political nemesis, it's to piece together the virtue behind what appears to be your nemesis's vice. In this respect, your goal is more like that of a therapist.

Visualizing the Virtue

Start with the soul-mate wisdom (see chapter 3, "Soul-Mate Wisdom #3") that every virtue taken to its extreme becomes a vice.

Before you can credibly visualize the virtue behind what you are likely to see only as the vice of extremist thought, it helps to understand how extremist thinking evolves from virtue to vice for all of us.

Extremist thinking almost always derives from an initial virtue such as the desire for prosperity the believer feels is best created by capitalism, or the desire for equality the believer feels is best created by socialism.

If their belief gains traction, groups of similarly minded people experience an emotional bond. Agreement stimulates the feel-good hormone of dopamine. Then when someone in that bonded group takes that virtue to the next step (e.g., free enterprise should never be regulated or everyone should have equal amounts of money), those who feel the bond become fearful that if they point out what they feel is a flaw, or if they even express hesitation, they'll risk losing the approval of the group.

This fear of stopping the virtue train on its way to "vice land" is significantly magnified if the group is being paid. Imagine a keynote speaker at an international convention of environmental scientists who presents the value of drilling oil in rural Alaska while green enhancements are still in the process of getting up to speed. Standing ovations are replaced with folded arms. Receptive minds close and myriad eyes ask are you really one of us? And vice versa for a keynote speaker at an international convention of oil companies who focuses on their damage to the environment.

When pay is involved, these executives' fear of collegial rejection is intensified by their fear of marring their reputation in their industry, distrust as a potential whistleblower, losing promotions, destroying their career, not being able to support their family, and feeling the daily emotional distance of colleagues who ignore them in the hall or leave them out of virtual meetings. These are just some of the social or financial bribes of closed-mindedness and polarization.

Examples of Visualizing the Virtue

Example #1: Imagine Being a Conservative Father Hearing Your Liberal Daughter

Imagine you are a politically conservative dad. You and your wife have worked for years to afford to send your daughter to college. She's home for her first Thanksgiving, and both of you can't wait to hear everything.

And she can't wait to share with you. You're delighted she's feeling so passionate until you hear that her passion is about advocating for reparations for Black Americans.

Well, in this case, before you argue first visualize the Love Guarantee and the other mindsets that are part of Alone Power with a family member.

Then after you've followed the mindsets, even if your daughter creates the space for you to respond, **search for the virtues that align with your values before you argue**. For example, before you argue that neither you, her mom, nor she owned a single slave, and not a single Black American person living in the US today was a slave so this is just liberal guilt money, and besides, giving huge amounts of money to people who don't directly earn it will only undermine incentives to achieve, which will reinforce the stereotype, **search for the virtues that align with your values**. In this example, some of the virtues might be:

Compassion: You and your daughter's mom likely taught your daughter the virtue of compassion. Focus first on how the advocacy for reparations reflects the virtue of compassion. Yes, you disagree with the solution of reparations, but focus first on the pride you have in her for going to college and thinking of something and someone other than herself.

Apologizing: You likely taught your daughter the importance of saying I'm sorry. Forget for a moment that you feel she has nothing to say I'm sorry about. Focus on the virtue: she is saying I'm sorry.

America as a Land of Equal Opportunity: You taught your daughter that people came to America because it is, more than any other country, a land of equal opportunity. Before you argue that reparations are not the path to equal opportunity, focus on the virtue of her desire to help America fulfill the ideal that you taught her it represents.

If she knows that you see how proud you are that she is committed to and inspired by the virtues you and her mom taught her, she'll more easily be able to hear how when taken to its extreme, those virtues can morph into vices.

Example #2: Imagine You Are That Liberal Daughter Hearing Your Conservative Dad

Imagine you are that daughter, and appreciation for the turkey is being replaced by disgust at your dad for passionately berating reparations for Black Americans.

Similarly, before you argue, first visualize the Love Guarantee and the other mindsets that are part of Alone Power with a family member.

Instead of arguing to the effect that any proposed reparations would account for but a tiny fraction of what the slave labor of African Americans contributed to the economic prosperity of the US; or that slaves were the only humans to come to the US whose hard labor did not lead to a better life for their children but only for the plantation owner; or that slaves were the only people who came to the US by force, not by choice; or that economic reparations could never even come close to repaying Black Americans for the premature deaths of their ancestors ... Before making these points in an argument, search for the virtues hidden in your dad's argument that align with your values. Here are some examples:

Equality of Opportunity: Consider how you want Black Americans to be equally motivated to work and succeed as other Americans, and that your dad's best intent is to give that motivation to Black Americans, but he feels that giving large sums of money to any individual may undermine that person's incentive to achieve and to perform at an equal level to White Americans. Consider that your dad, like you, doesn't want to reinforce the worst stereotypes. You don't have to agree with your dad's conclusion in order to search for a virtue that may motivate your dad: equality of opportunity.

Self-Respect: Your dad and you will doubtless align with the desire for everyone to have self-respect. The result of the GI Bill for millions of veterans of World War II was that every GI except those who were

Black was given a free college education, which usually increased self-respect and respect from others; provided interest-free home loans, which usually also increased self-respect; and landed them in the middle class and invested in society's rules that similarly increased both respect from others and self-respect. Black Americans were deprived of all these pathways to self-respect via the GI Bill. Rather than focus on these points as a loss of money that needs to be given back via reparations, focus on the self-respect virtue with which you and your dad will align.

What Does All This Alignment of Virtues Allow For?

Once dad and daughter can see their alignment on core virtues such as compassion, equality of opportunity, and self-respect, they can leave the Thanksgiving table with thanks that their dad or daughter saw the virtue behind their perspective rather than seeing their college money being used as poison or their dad being poison. And that's enough of a gift to be worthy of their mutual thanks.

If they have incorporated that respect for each other, they have the choice to take it a step further, to explore together alternative paths to equality of opportunity. For example, since Black American veterans were excluded from the GI Bill's benefits of free college and interest-free home loans, Dad may understand how the much more recent example of clear inequality should be compensated for by offering Black Americans today what allowed so many White veterans to move into the middle class yesterday: a free college education and interest-free home loans. A solution such as that would also create more taxpayers rather than welfare recipients. Conversely, the daughter can easily see how this is a type of reparation that would give Black Americans the equalities of opportunity and self-respect she hoped for.

It is only because the daughter and dad could experience each other aligned on core virtues rather than focusing on dad-the-racist or daughter-the-enabler that they could respectfully brainstorm solutions with or without agreement. The family can then look forward to their next holiday dinner: an exciting civil dialogue with family rather than a civil war, with Tums.

Alone Power is so crucial because it is unlikely that the discipline it takes to make the evolutionary shift from civil war to civil dialogue is likely to occur for more than a tiny percentage of people in our lifetime. Alone Power allows you to share the gift of being heard and seen with everyone you encounter.

Conclusion

O vercoming the barriers to deeper love takes more than reading *Role Mate to Soul Mate*; it takes practicing it. Similarly, the online video course is effective not in the viewing but in the doing.* This is because the Achilles' heel of humans is our inability to handle personal criticism from a loved one without becoming defensive.

Two factors are the biggest contributors to a deeper love. Together, they require making nothing less than an evolutionary shift. First, historically, our Achilles' heel of defensiveness was functional: When a nearby tribe or country criticized us, we feared a potential enemy, and therefore it was functional for survival to respond to criticism by immediately erecting defenses. However, what was functional for survival is dysfunctional for love.

Second, since falling in love is biologically natural, and both sustaining and deepening a soul mate–type love is biologically unnatural, the shift from role mate to soul mate requires an evolutionary shift. This book offers 23 Love Enhancements to make this shift. All 23 are *un*natural, and

---

* https://communication.warrenfarrell.com/role-mate-to-soul-mate-course/

therefore it requires discipline to do and repeat these Love Enhancements until they come naturally.

While all 23 of the Love Enhancements are meant to fit like pieces in the puzzle of the transition from role mate to soul mate, you'll see a great transformation simply by repeatedly practicing the first three of the seven secrets to a deeper love:

1. Pan for your partner's gold for specific appreciations that can refill your reservoir of love.
2. Practice the Caring and Sharing's 24 steps each week.
3. Create and sustain the Conflict-Free Zone especially by responding to criticism by visualizing waiting for a Caring and Sharing session to be heard rather than responding immediately and being hurt.

The three wisdoms that I've seen serving couples best once the reasons for them are understood are:

First, why criticism looks different to the criticizer and the criticized.

Second, why anger is vulnerability's mask.

Third, why the secret to feeling loved is feeling understood: why no one says, "I want a divorce, my partner understands me."

While the 23 Love Enhancements deepen love for all couples whether heterosexual or same-sex, they are of particular value for couples raising children. Raising children and dealing with monetary and time constraints magnify a couple's problems even as those problems become the reason a couple stays together. Enter the minimum-security-prison marriage.

Ironically, when parents have the least time for the Love Enhancements, they have the greatest need. Yet it doesn't take long for the Love Enhancements to save parents more time than they consume just as a well-maintained car saves more time than a poorly maintained car stranded in "anger land."

Whether raising children or not, the process never ends. Liz and I both work hard. We are still learning to play more and make better use of our music to dance more whether spontaneously and joyfully, or romantically and soulfully.

Is it worth it? Well, in one sense it's like having children: it's the hardest work you'll ever do (and the parenting process never ends), but the depth of love taps into our soul at a level that makes the great majority of couples experience a happiness and love they had never known before. For most parents, the hard work is more than worth the rewards of love.

Fortunately, there's even better news for your transition from role mate to soul mate. While the multiple steps of the Caring and Sharing Practice can be a pain in the neck, I'm told it's not nearly as painful as having a child! And that's just the starter benefit.

In the 30 years of conducting the "Role Mate to Soul Mate" workshops, the majority of couples report that even after just one Caring and Sharing session of being fully heard about something they've previously said a hundred times without being fully heard, leaves them knowing they can experience this feeling again at any time. Even if they fail to do the Caring and Sharing Practice the next week, they feel the internal security of knowing they have the process in writing and on video for any moment in the future.

Our reservoir of love will always experience periods of depletion. What is biologically natural creeps back. It is more natural to blame than to take responsibility. Instead, replace the blame with renewing your discipline: check in on the role of the Four Lazinesses in creating the Four Depleters of Love; do all the stages of journaling to revive the Conflict-Free Zone; recall Alone Power and Hold to replace defensiveness with Caring and Sharing sessions; feel the vulnerability beneath your partner's anger; add to your relational feng shui; design a creative and specific appreciation; practice creating win-win solutions for your stickiest problems; anticipate a Four-Part Apology; substitute Asks for criticisms. Doing just a few of those will allow your partner to feel it is safe to take off their armor and begin to risk their heart again.

If you are feeling a disconnect about any issue from personal to political with someone in your family, a friend, or colleague, review the chapter on civil war to civil dialogue and rediscover how to use Alone Power to search for the best intent and original virtues from which views with which you now disagree may have emanated from virtues with which you can align.

As *Role Mate to Soul Mate* enhances you and your partner's communication, your children will begin to unconsciously absorb it and apply it to their siblings, friends, and soon to their romantic partners. However, FDNs that follow the guidelines to prevent them from becoming family dinner nightmares will allow your children to have the unconscious become conscious. They will attract higher quality friends. Some will become teachers of the process.*

Role Mate to Soul Mate is designed to both deepen love and provide an omnipresent and specific structure to help you rebuild love that has suffered from the natural responses of defensiveness and anger. It is like having a gym in your own home with a coach on call 24-7. As you revive the Art and Discipline of Love, you will give yourself the ticket of readmission to your loved one's soul; you will recapture the magic that first drew you together.

Each time you revisit the book or video, you will experience it from an evolved perspective. You'll notice insights that perhaps didn't resonate with you before but that you now feel ready to integrate. You'll connect

---

* If you or your children wish to become certified trainers in these Role Mate to Soul Mate methods, email me at warren@warrenfarrell.com.

the dots you might have missed earlier. As you add the new depth to your practice, you'll feel the new depth to your love.

Your journey is not just about reaching a destination. It's about the journey itself—the bittersweet symphony of shared experiences, the dance of differences and compromises, the melody of love that binds us together. It is not a journey that defines us; it is a journey that refines us.

Role Mate to Soul Mate, then, is a journey not for the fainthearted. It is for those who dare to alter their relationship DNA from the survival defensiveness of role mate to one that thrives in soil enriched by the 23 Love Enhancements, nurtured by being fully heard, pruned by honesty, watered with wisdom, warmed by specific appreciations, and fertilized by the art and discipline that together create the enduring love of a soul mate.

Appendix

How this book's online video course facilitates your mastery of the 23 Love Enhancements

've been honest that the most a book can do is to impart wisdom, but that when criticism appears, wisdom disappears. The best way to incorporate the wisdom of the 23 Love Enhancements into your life is to practice the exercises with your partner. This is much more easily done with the online video version than with the book alone.

The video course shows me working with two couples as they go through the process. By pausing the video as the other couples do an exercise, you'll be able to go through the process with them and watch me resolve the stumbling blocks the couples encounter. It's a lot like being in the workshop in person.

A second challenge: We've seen how falling in love is biologically natural, but that sustaining love is biologically unnatural. Which is why this practice requires the discipline of doing it repeatedly until your brain's natural response of defensiveness in response to criticism slowly changes to incorporate more naturally the 23 Love Enhancements. The online video allows you to practice this as often as you need until your brain incorporates these love enhancements naturally (well, *almost* naturally!).

Finally, if you have children, they may never read this book. You and your partner's communication style will be their book.

The QR code makes the video available at more than a 50 percent discount ($97). By buying the book, you save $100.

Email me at warren@warrenfarrell.com if:

1. The course doesn't deepen your love, and I will return your money.
2. You wish to become a **certified trainer**.
3. You would like to help distribute the online course to **poor communities** for free.

For an **in-person workshop**, see the Couples' Communication tab at www.warrenfarrell.com.

Notes

1. Saul McLeod, "Maslow's Hierarchy of Needs," *Simply Psychology*, 2017, https://www.simplypsychology.org/maslow.html.
2. Jo A. Iodice, John M. Malouff, and Nicola S. Schutte, "The Association between Gratitude and Depression: A Meta-Analysis," *International Journal of Depression and Anxiety* 4, no. 1 (2021): 24, https://doi.org/10.23937/2643 -4059/1710024.
3. Dacher Keltner, "In Defense of Teasing," *New York Times Magazine*, December 5, 2008, http://www.nytimes.com/2008/12/07/magazine/07teasing-t.html.
4. Richard Fletcher, University of Newcastle, Australia, et al., as cited in Sue Shellenbarger, "Roughhousing Lessons from Dad: Fathers Teach Risk-Taking, Boundary-Setting; Learning From 'Sock Wrestling,'" *Wall Street Journal*, updated June 11, 2014, https://www.wsj.com/articles/roughhousing -lessons-from-dad-1402444262.
5. Richard Fletcher, University of Newcastle, Australia, et al., as cited in Sue Shellenbarger, "Roughhousing Lessons from Dad: Fathers Teach Risk-Taking, Boundary-Setting; Learning From 'Sock Wrestling,'" *Wall Street Journal*, updated June 11, 2014, https://www.wsj.com/articles/roughhousing -lessons-from-dad-1402444262.
6. Richard Koestner, C. Franz, and J. Weinberger, "The Family Origins of Empathic Concern: A Twenty-Six-Year Longitudinal Study," *Journal of Personality and Social Psychology* 58, no. 4 (April 1990): 709–17.

Bibliography

Blankenhorn, David. *In Search of Braver Angels.* (New York, N.Y.: Braver Angels, 2022)

Brooks, David. *How to Know a Person: The Art of Seeing Others Deeply and Being Deeply Seen* (New York: Random House, 2023).

Canfield, Jack & Watkins, D.D. *Jack Canfield's Key to Living the Law of Attraction: A Simple Guide to Creating the Life of Your Dreams* (Deerfield: Health Communications Inc., 2007).

Farrell, Warren. *The Boy Crisis: Why Our Boys are Struggling and What We Can Do About It* (Dallas: BenBella Books, 2018)

Gottman, John. *The Seven Principles for Making Marriage Work: A Practical Guide from the Country's Foremost Relationship Expert* (New York: Harmony, 2015).

Gottman, John & Schwartz Gottman, Julie. *Eight Dates: Essential Conversations for a Lifetime of Love* (New York: Workman Publishing Company, 2019).

Gray, John. *Men Are from Mars, Women Are from Venus: The Classic Guide to Understanding the Opposite Sex* (New York: Harper Paperbacks, 2012).

Hendricks, Gay & Hendricks, Kathlyn. *Conscious Loving: The Journey to Co-Commitment* (New York: Bantam Books, 1992).

Hendrix, Harville & Hunt Helen. *Getting the Love You Want: A Guide for Couples: Third Edition* (New York: St. Martin's Griffin, 2019).

Perel, Ester. *Mating in Captivity: Unlocking Erotic Intelligence* (New York: Harper Paperbacks, 2017).

Shimoff, Marci. *Love for No Reason: 7 Steps to Creating a Life of Unconditional Love* (New York: Atria Books, 2010).

Index

Index

About the Author

Dr. **Warren Farrell** has coached couples and psychologists nationwide in couples' communication for the past 30 years. His courses, both live and the online video versions, are also titled *Role Mate to Soul Mate.*

Dr. Farrell has been chosen by the *Financial Times* of London as one of the world's top 100 thought leaders. His books are published in 19 languages. They include the *New York Times* best-seller, *Why Men Are the Way They Are,* plus the international best-seller, *The Myth of Male Power.* His previous book on couple's communication, *Women Can't Hear What Men Don't Say,* was a selection of the Book of the Month Club. His most recent book is *The Boy Crisis.*

Warren Farrell has been a pioneer in both the women's movement (elected three times to the board of the National Organization for Women in New York City) and the men's movement (called by *GQ* magazine "The Martin Luther King of the men's movement"). He has been interviewed by Oprah, Barbara Walters, Peter Jennings, Sean Hannity, Katie Couric, Larry King, Tucker Carlson, Regis Philbin, Jordan Peterson, and Charlie Rose. He has frequently written for and been featured in the *New York Times* and publications worldwide. Dr. Farrell has two daughters, lives with his wife in Mill Valley, California, and virtually at www.warrenfarrell.com.